FROM- Aunt Irene '92

ORIENTAL
APPETIZERS

by the same authors

JAPANESE GARNISHES

MORE JAPANESE
GARNISHES

YUKIKO AND BOB HAYDOCK

ORIENTAL APPETIZERS

HOLT, RINEHART AND WINSTON · NEW YORK

Copyright © 1984 by Yukiko and Bob Haydock
All rights reserved, including the right to reproduce
this book or portions thereof in any form.
Published by Holt, Rinehart and Winston,
383 Madison Avenue, New York, New York 10017.
Published simultaneously in Canada by Holt, Rinehart
and Winston of Canada, Limited.

Library of Congress Cataloging in Publication Data
Haydock, Yukiko.
Oriental appetizers.
1. Cookery (Appetizers)   2. Cookery, Oriental.
I. Haydock, Bob.   II. Title.
TX740.H3 1984   641.8′12   83-12887
ISBN 0-03-063558-6

First Edition

Printed in the United States of America
10 9 8 7 6 5 4 3 2 1

ISBN 0-03-063558-6

CONTENTS

Others

Sauces, Dips, and Dough

FOREWORD

In 1949 my husband was appointed commercial attaché to the Chinese Mission in Japan. We left Shanghai together, not knowing that our plane was to be the last one permitted out of that city, or that for over twenty-five years it would be impossible to return. The Red Army under Mao Tse-tung had won the country, and would forever change the way of life of Chinese society.

I also did not dream that Tokyo would mean the beginning of a new life for me as a restaurant proprietress. In those early days of the occupation there was only one small Chinese restaurant in Tokyo. So some friends and I decided to venture into the restaurant business. With the help of excellent chefs brought from Hong Kong, we were immediately successful, not only with the Chinese community, but also with the Japanese. The restaurant prospered, and I continued to operate it until 1961 when a widowed sister asked me to join her in San Francisco.

Once again I found myself in a new country, and once again had no thought of opening a restaurant. But fate proved to be a better guide. Before long, friends urged me to take over an establishment on Polk Street whose owner wanted to sell. I finally decided to gamble, because I realized that although there were hundreds of Chinese restaurants in San Francisco, none served the hot, spicy cuisine of the Mandarin classes of Northern China. With this approach, I returned to the restaurant business and had the good fortune to repeat my Tokyo success.

After a few years I began noticing a young couple who returned to the restaurant often. Of course, they were Yukiko and Bob Haydock, and were thoroughly enjoying the Northern cuisine that we had brought to the Bay Area. We began a long friendship, and later, when I moved my restaurant, The Mandarin, to Ghirardelli Square and decided to give weekly cooking classes, I asked Yukiko to assist me. With the class we had great fun trying out many of the traditional dishes of old Mandarin China.

Naturally, the appetizer was an important part of our culinary syllabus. The appetizer seems more significant in the cuisines of Asia than in the West. Perhaps it is because alcohol has never been regarded as the primary reason for getting together as it is at the western cocktail party. It is always the food first, with the alcohol in pleasant accompaniment.

But perhaps the greatest reason for the profusion of appetizers is the multitude of rites and ceremonies that inspire them, such as New Year's, which in China lasts for fifteen days. Houses are thrown open to relatives and friends who flow in and out. Teas and delicacies are served to all comers. Houses are bright with colorful decorations, and dinner parties are given by all to be attended in your finest new clothes. Lucky poems are written and relatives give presents of money wrapped in red paper. Wedding dinners are yet another grand occasion when the appetizers are most elaborate. And, of course, funerals too, which bring together many relatives. In less formal circumstances, during free periods at school, I can vividly remember running out to buy onion cakes from the everpresent street vendors whose portable kitchens held dozens of flavorful snacks. And, of course, the Mah Jong party always produces a nice sampling of savory treats to nervously wash down with your choice of tea while your purse swells or depletes itself.

I think the essence of the tiny appetizer can best be expressed by a judgment my father made about food. He was a slight man, not a large eater, but he always enjoyed the best food. He held the view that if one ate the best, one did not need to eat so much.

—CECILIA SUN YUNG CHIANG
author of *The Mandarin Way*
owner of The Mandarin restaurants in San Francisco and
Beverly Hills, California

INTRODUCTION

There is a story about the origin of Chinese appetizers that we would like to retell here. We have no way of knowing how true this story is, but we want to repeat it because it sets just the right adventurous, experimental mood for a book on oriental appetizers. As the story goes, a thousand years ago a Sung dynasty emperor with an adventurous palate insisted that his chefs continually develop new and exciting delicacies for his table. His insatiable demands for variety made it impossible for his chefs to cook, or for him to consume, full meals. So they hit upon the idea of preparing innumerable bite-size portions. These little experiments later developed into the Chinese culinary art of dim sum.

This is exactly what an appetizer should be—a tasty little experiment to delight you. It should perk up your interest in what is to come. Of course, imperial delicacies like larks' tongues or bear's palms aren't always available in the local supermarkets. So this book confines itself to the more modest delights from the homes, restaurants, and street-corner food carts of Asia.

As world cultures intermingle, so do their foods. Herbs, spices, fish sauces, and shrimp pastes that were once rare and unfamiliar in the West are now appearing in chain supermarkets. A notable example is tōfu, the soybean cake. Unknown and ignored a few years ago, tōfu has now been the subject of a number of popular cookbooks, and is available almost everywhere. This means that oriental cookbooks, which of necessity depend upon less well-known ingredients, are now becoming practical as the ingredients themselves become available and familiar. This promises great new taste experiences for us all. We hope that experimenting with oriental appetizers can be a way for you and your guests to enjoy some of those experiences.

INGREDIENTS

Bamboo Shoots. Bamboo shoots are quite common in oriental cooking. For our purposes the canned water-packed variety is good. Once opened they should be used as soon as possible. They can be stored in fresh water in the refrigerator for about a week if the water is changed daily.

Breadcrumbs. There are numerous brands of packaged breadcrumbs on the market. We recommend that you investigate Japanese style breadcrumbs (panko). They are much coarser than the western brands and therefore produce a much crisper coating.

Chili Peppers. A number of hot chili peppers are on the market. They are used throughout Asia as flavorings to add heat to sauces. They range from mildly hot to ferocious. We use the fresh, unpickled kind, about 2 to 2½ inches long. The seeds, which are very hot, are usually removed. Care should be taken when handling chilies, since the oil can irritate the skin and be accidentally rubbed into the eyes.

Chinese Cabbage. May also be called napa cabbage, pe-tsai (Chinese) or hakusai (Japanese) cabbage. The leaves are more tender and have a much milder flavor than other cabbage. The cabbage grows in an elongated shape rather than the conventional round ball shape. Although they were originally used almost exclusively by the oriental community, they are now quite widely sold.

Coconut Milk. Not to be mistaken for the thin water found in the fresh whole coconut. Coconut milk is extracted from the white coconut meat. It is a rather thick creamy white liquid.

Coriander. Although coriander is also known as Chinese parsley, conventional parsley is not a substitute. The flavors are entirely different. If coriander isn't available in your market, a small packet of seeds available at most nurseries will yield an abundant fresh supply when planted in a sunny area.

Corn Flour. Comes from milling corn. It is a finer version of corn meal. It may be either white or yellow, depending upon the corn used. Available at health food stores.

Curry Powder. We recommend the use of packaged curry powder because it is readily available at supermarket spice racks. Of course, grinding up your own dried spices is the best way. Usually curry powder is a combination of about fifteen spices such as allspice, anise, bay leaves, dill, ginger, etc. Turmeric is one of the dominant spices. It provides the yellow color and the familiar curry flavor.

Dried Shrimp. Dried shrimp are used as a flavoring agent in oriental cooking. They impart a concentrated salty, shrimp flavor to food. Small shrimps are salted, shelled, and dried. They are sold by the pound in oriental markets. They can be stored indefinitely in the refrigerator in a closed jar.

Dried Shrimp Paste. Many countries in Asia produce this powerful, odorous paste from prawns. In America the two most common names are kapi (Thailand) or blachen (Malaysia). It is imported either in cans or in hard cakes. Neither needs refrigeration.

Eggplant (Japanese). The Japanese eggplant is much smaller (5 to 8 inches) and more flavorful than the American varieties. It also has fewer seeds and they are very tender so they are easily eaten.

Egg Roll Wrappers. Packaged egg roll wrappers are commonly available in markets. They should not be confused with spring roll wrappers which are much thinner and contain no egg.

Five Spice Powder. A very strong, reddish brown powder that is very important in Chinese cooking. It is usually sold in boxes in oriental food stores. Buy the smallest amount possible. It will last a long time. The powder is a combination of ground Szechwan peppercorns, anise, fennel, cloves, and cinnamon.

Garam Masala. A mixture of good quality ground spices such as cumin, coriander, peppercorns, cinnamon, cloves, etc. It is used primarily in Indian cooking. Packaged garam masala is available in specialty food stores.

Garlic. Garlic is as well known and widely used in Asia as it is in the rest of the world. It is a perennial plant cultivated for the strong smelling bulb. Garlic powder should never be used as a substitute.

Ginger Root. Always use the fresh ginger root. It is readily available. Ginger powder or dried ginger cannot match its zesty, spicy taste. Ginger juice is made simply by extracting the juice from a small piece of fresh ginger with a garlic press. Pickled ginger root is packaged in jars and is available in oriental markets. It is vinegared and usually dyed a bright cherry red. For this reason it makes an excellent garnish.

Ground Bean Sauce. A salty brown sauce made from soybeans. It can be used as a base for other sauces. It is sold in cans.

Hoisin Sauce. A thick, sweet, tangy sauce made from soybeans, sugar, garlic, and spices. It is indispensable as a sauce for Peking Duck. Anyone who has enjoyed that dish will immediately know the sauce. Chefs often mix the sauce half and half with ground bean sauce to make it milder.

Lard. Lard is an age-old cooking fat used in many parts of Asia. It is obtained by melting down pork fat. The richness of flavor it imparts to food cooked in it is almost irresistible. But if for health reasons, the irresistible has to be resisted, a light vegetable oil may be substituted.

Lemon Grass. A grass-type plant that is used to impart a lemony flavor to food. For a long time, lemon grass was not available in United States markets; however, it has begun to appear in recent years. A couple of strips of lemon rind may be substituted.

Mirin. A heavy sweetened Japanese sake with an alcohol content of about 14 percent. It is used exclusively for cooking, often as a sweetener or basting liquid.

Miso. One of Japan's most important and widely consumed foods. It is not much of an exaggeration to say that every Japanese eats some form of miso every day, either in soup or in a variety of other combinations. Miso is made from cooked, fermented soybeans. Broadly speaking it falls into three types—light, red, and dark.

Nam Pla. A salty fish sauce used much in the way that soy sauce is used to enhance the flavor of other foods. Nam pla is the Thai name for the sauce, but it is generally used throughout Southeast Asia.

Nori. A dark brown seaweed that is collected from the ocean, washed, and dried in thin sheets. Nori is probably best known in America as a wrapping for sushi. Nori can be kept by wrapping in plastic wrap and storing in an airtight can. Nori is very sensitive to humidity and will lose its crispness if not protected.

Oyster Sauce. Oyster sauce is sold in bottles. It is commonly available at supermarkets these days. It is a viscous brown sauce made by cooking oysters in soy sauce and salt water.

Palm Sugar. May be purchased either in canned or brick form. We are using it in the canned, soft form. It is the boiled down, crystallized sap of the coconut palm. Brown sugar may be substituted.

Rice Flour. A white, powdery flourlike substance made from ground rice. Used in making rice noodles and pastry. Available in oriental specialty stores. Not to be confused with sweet rice flour, which is made from glutinous rice or sweet rice.

Rice Vinegar. In the Orient, vinegar is generally produced from rice. It is milder and sweeter than Western vinegar. It is becoming well known in America and can be found in most supermarkets.

Sake. The comparatively inexpensive, fairly strong (19 percent alcohol) Japanese rice wine. Sake is one of the main flavoring ingredients in Japanese cuisine.

Sansho Powder. The ground pod of the sansho tree. It is used as a seasoning over fish or chicken. But it is enjoyed more for the fragrance that it imparts to the dish than for the actual taste.

Semolina. A coarsely milled wheat product often used in puddings and soups.

Sesame Seeds. Used in many parts of Asia mostly as a coating for sweets and other foods. Both black and white seeds are available. The color choice depends mainly on the accent desired rather than the taste.

Sesame Seed Oil. A strongly flavored oil derived from toasted sesame seeds. It is used primarily for flavoring rather than cooking.

Shiitake Mushrooms. Mushrooms cultivated on the bark of the shii tree and other trees of the oak family. Shiitake can be purchased either fresh or dried. Shiitake are popular ingredients in oriental cooking because they are flavorful and quite easy to grow commercially.

Soy Sauce. A salty, brown sauce made by naturally fermenting soybeans, wheat, and salt. Soy sauce comes in both light and dark varieties as well as a low salt (salt content reduced to 8.8 percent from 14.8 percent) product. Light soy sauce is generally used with lighter colored foods.

Spring Roll Wrappers. These wrappers differ from egg roll wrappers in that they are a lot thinner and contain no egg. This produces a lighter, crispier, almost translucent wrapper when fried.

Star Anise. The dried pod of the anise plant. It is sold whole in oriental specialty stores. It resembles an eight-pointed star and has the characteristic anise licorice flavor.

Tamarind Water. The liquid resulting from soaking the dried tamarind seed with hot water. Tamarind water is bottled and can be purchased in oriental markets. It is also used extensively in Latin America, so Latin markets are also a source.

Tapioca Starch. A white flourlike substance made from grinding cassava root starch. It is used as a sauce thickener. It is also favored for

making dim sum wrappers because it produces a crisp texture.

Tōfu. The soybean yields up three important products for Asia—miso, shōyu (soy sauce), and tōfu. The milk of the soybean is coagulated to create curds, which are poured into large rectangular molds. American supermarkets sell tōfu packed in water in small sealed plastic tubs. Tōfu should always be kept floating in water and refrigerated. The water should be changed daily.

Turmeric. An East Indian plant whose powdered root is used as a yellow dye, as well as a seasoning. It is one of the key spices in curry powder.

Wasabi Powder. A green powdered Japanese horseradish with a sharp taste and smell. It is sold in cans and is reconstituted with water in the same manner as dry mustard.

Wheat Starch. The residue of wheat flour after protein removal. It is sold by the pound in Chinese grocery stores. It can be stored in the same manner as flour.

DEEP FRIED

CHICKEN CRISPS

Japan

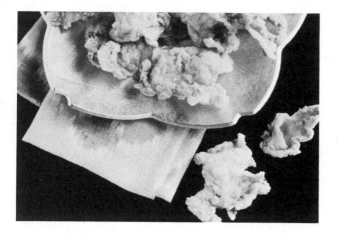

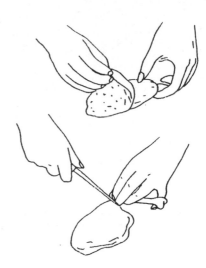

1. Remove skin and bone the chicken thighs. Cover and freeze for 2 to 3 hours to prepare meat for thin slicing.

TECHNIQUES
Just before serving, drop the appetizers back into hot oil for 20 to 30 seconds or until golden brown. Serve hot.

2. Slice frozen thighs at an angle into ⅛-inch-thick slices as shown. Place the slices in a bowl and sprinkle with salt, pepper, and curry powder. Mix well and set aside for ten minutes.

Serves 8

4 chicken thighs
½ teaspoon salt
¼ teaspoon freshly
    ground pepper
¼ teaspoon curry
    powder
Cornstarch
Wax paper
Oil for deep frying

3. Dust the pieces with cornstarch and place on a sheet of wax paper.

4. Cover with another piece of wax paper and pound the chicken into paper-thin wafers with the flat side of a mallet.

5. Remove the top piece of wax paper. Carefully loosen each wafer from the bottom sheet of wax paper.

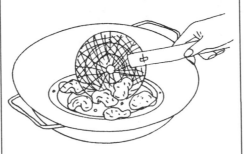

6. Heat oil in a wok or deep fryer to 325° F. and fry chicken a few pieces at a time until light brown, about 1½ to 2 minutes. Drain on a rack.

3

CHICKEN NORIMAKI

Japan

1. Skin, bone, and mince the chicken. Peel the carrot and cook until just tender. Mince. Blanch the string beans. Mince.

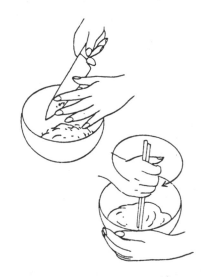

TECHNIQUES
Light soy sauce is used to preserve the light color of the chicken. In Step 6, cooling before slicing helps to keep the juices from running out.

2. Combine all of the ingredients except nori and oil in a bowl and mix until they become tacky and pasty.

3. Place a sheet of nori on a bamboo mat (maki sudare). Put ⅓ of the chicken mixture along the nori's edge closest to you.

4. Using your finger, moisten the other edge with a little chicken mixture. Using the bamboo mat to aid you, gently roll up the nori and seal with the moist end.

5. Heat 2 inches of oil in a wok or skillet to a moderately low temperature. Slip the norimake in and fry for about 4 minutes. It is done if it feels firm when squeezed with tongs. Remove and drain on several thicknesses of paper towel. Repeat with remaining chicken mixture and remaining 2 sheets of nori.

6. Cool for 10 minutes. Cut into ¾-inch slices. Serve at room temperature.

To make about 30

1 whole chicken breast, skinned, boned, and minced
½ carrot, peeled, cooked until just tender, and minced
¼ cup minced onion
4 string beans, blanched and minced
2 teaspoons fresh ginger juice
1 tablespoon light soy sauce (if not available, use regular)
1 egg, lightly beaten
3 sheets nori (seaweed)
Oil for deep frying

5

CHICKEN TATTA AGE

Japan

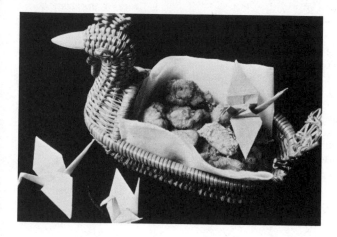

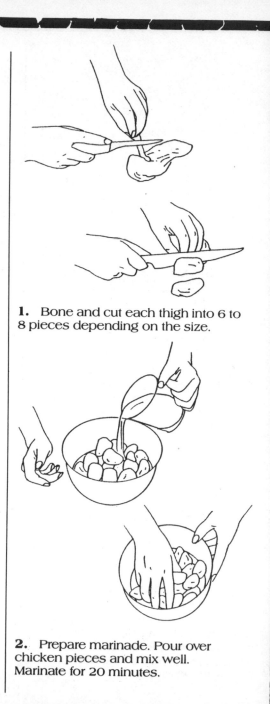

1. Bone and cut each thigh into 6 to 8 pieces depending on the size.

2. Prepare marinade. Pour over chicken pieces and mix well. Marinate for 20 minutes.

3. Mix flour and cornstarch thoroughly in a bowl. Coat the chicken with the mixture and dust off excess.

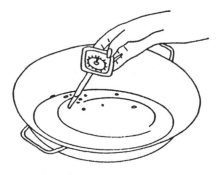

4. Heat oil in a wok or deep fryer to 325° F. Fry the chicken for 2 to 2½ minutes. Be careful to regulate the heat. The chicken is easily burned because of the soy sauce in the marinade.

4 chicken thighs

Marinade
2½ tablespoons soy
    sauce
1 tablespoon mirin
½ teaspoon ginger root
    juice
½ cup flour
½ cup cornstarch
Oil for deep frying

CRAB AND TŌFU BALLS

Japan

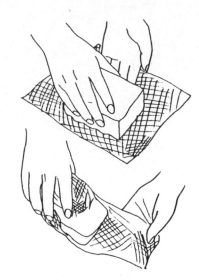

1. Remove the tōfu from its container and place on a piece of cheesecloth. Wrap the tōfu.

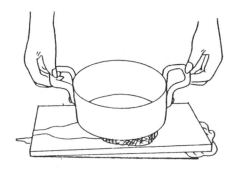

2. Place the tōfu on a tilted cutting board next to the sink. Place a weight such as a large pot on top of it. This presses excess water from the tōfu. The water will drain down the slanted board into the sink. Press for 30 minutes.

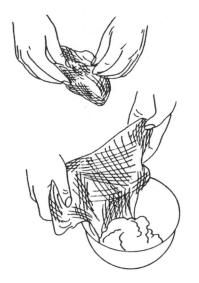

3. Mash the tōfu with fingers and empty into a mixing bowl.

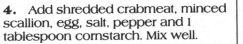

4. Add shredded crabmeat, minced scallion, egg, salt, pepper and 1 tablespoon cornstarch. Mix well.

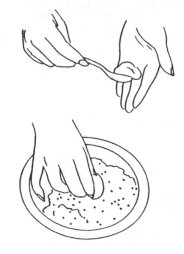

5. Take a tablespoon of the mixture in the palm and roll into a small ball. Roll in cornstarch. Repeat with the remainder of the mixture.

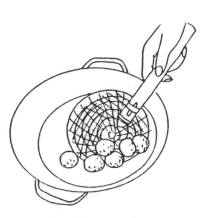

6. Drop into deep hot oil (375° F.) and fry until golden brown. Serve the balls as they are or with tempura sauce, soy sauce mixed with hot mustard, or mayonnaise mixed with horseradish.

To make about 24

1 16-ounce container
    Japanese style tōfu
    (soybean cake)
¼ pound cooked
    crabmeat, shredded
1 scallion, minced
1 egg, beaten
½ teaspoon salt
¼ teaspoon pepper
1 cup cornstarch
Oil for deep frying

9

FIVE SPICE SPARERIBS

China

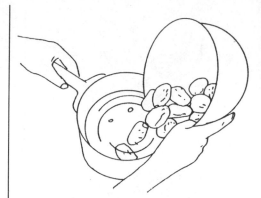

1. Cook spareribs in boiling water sufficient to cover them for 10 minutes. Skim off fat when necessary. Add scallion, ginger, star anise, sherry, salt, sugar, and soy sauce. Cover and continue to cook for 20 to 25 minutes, stirring occasionally.

2. Remove ribs with a strainer and sprinkle thoroughly with cornstarch. Set aside to cool completely. The ribs can be prepared ahead up to this point and refrigerated until ready to fry.

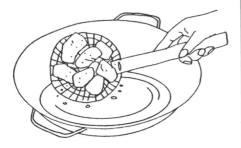

3. Drop ribs into deep hot oil (medium high heat) and fry for 5 minutes or until they are golden brown. Remove and drain.

4. Sprinkle with Five Spice Salt (page 136) and serve.

To serve 8

2 pounds backrib style
    spareribs
2 stalks large whole
    scallion
1 thumb-size ginger
    root, lightly mashed
5 whole star anise
3 tablespoons sherry
1 teaspoon salt
3 teaspoons sugar
3 tablespoons soy
    sauce
½ cup cornstarch
Oil for deep frying
1 teaspoon Five Spice
    Salt (page 136)

FRIED CHICKEN WINGS

India

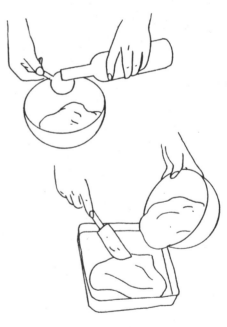

1. Cut the chicken wings at the joints and discard tips. Prick the skin to allow marinade to penetrate.

2. Mix together the marinade ingredients and pour it out into a glass or enameled pan or large, shallow bowl.

3. Place the wings in the marinade, being sure they are all covered. Marinate for at least 24 hours.

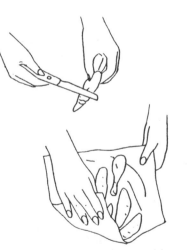

4. Scrape off the marinade and pat dry with paper toweling.

5. Heat oil in a wok or frying pan and deep fry the chicken pieces.

To make 40

20 chicken wings

Marinade
2½ cups yogurt
½ cup catsup
2 cloves garlic, puréed
2 teaspoons grated
   fresh ginger root
½ onion, grated
Juice of 1 lemon
2 teaspoons curry
   powder
½ teaspoon cayenne
   pepper
2 tablespoons cumin
2 tablespoons
   coriander
2 tablespoons paprika
1 teaspoon cardamom
½ teaspoon pepper
½ teaspoon nutmeg
½ teaspoon cinnamon
½ teaspoon mace
5 tablespoons olive oil
1 tablespoon salt

Oil for deep frying

FRIED FISHCAKE

Thailand

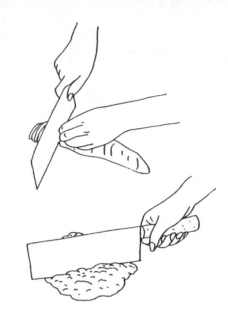

1. Cut up and then chop the fish fillet very fine. Place in a mortar and grind until it reaches a pastelike consistency.

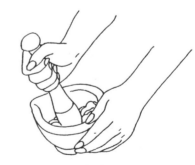

2. Remove fish. Again in a mortar grind together shallots, garlic, lemon grass, coriander root, ginger root, and shrimp paste.

TECHNIQUES
Step 1 should not be done with a food processor. Thorough chopping with a cleaver, as shown, will preserve the texture of the meat. This is often done with two cleavers, one in each hand.

3. Combine fish, green beans, ground seasonings, and pepper, optional chili, sugar, and salt together in a bowl. Mix eggs into the paste.

4. Shape the mixture into balls.

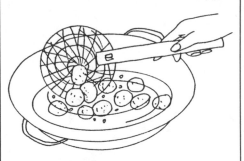

5. Heat oil in a wok to 325° F. Fry until golden.

6. To make dipping sauce, combine all the ingredients for the dipping sauce in a small saucepan and cook, stirring constantly, until sauce thickens slightly and becomes slightly transparent.

To serve 8

½ lb red snapper fillet
2 tablespoons minced
   shallots
1 teaspoon minced
   garlic
2 tablespoons minced
   lemon grass
1 teaspoon minced
   fresh coriander root
1 teaspoon minced
   fresh ginger root
1 teaspoon dried
   shrimp paste
2 ounces thinly sliced
   green beans
¼ teaspoon ground
   black pepper
½ teaspoon crushed
   chili (optional)
½ teaspoon sugar
½ teaspoon salt
2 eggs, lightly beaten
Oil for frying

Dipping Sauce
3 tablespoons lime
   juice
2 tablespoons sugar
1 tablespoon soy sauce
3 teaspoons cornstarch
¼ cup water

15

FRIED SQUID RINGS

China

1. Sift together cornstarch, flour, baking soda, and salt. Lightly beat egg and add. Add vinegar and oil. Add water and thoroughly mix batter until smooth. Set aside for 30 minutes at room temperature.

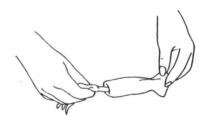

2. Pull the tentacles from the squid. The quill and innards should come out with the tentacles. Clean out any remaining innards and discard. Pull skin off.

TECHNIQUES
Be sure to follow the cleaning instructions. Pieces of the quill can remain on the rings and be an annoyance when eating—somewhat like fish scales on an improperly cleaned fish.

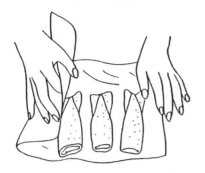

3. Wash the bodies inside and out under running water. At this time be sure all of the innards have been removed, especially any remaining pieces of the quill. Pat dry with paper towel inside and out.

5. Heat oil to 350° F. Put the squid rings into the batter several pieces at a time to coat.

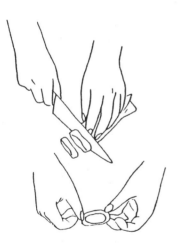

4. Cut the bodies into ½-inch-wide rings as shown. Thoroughly pat dry again with paper towel.

6. Drop into the hot oil one by one, cooking several at once. Fry only for 45 seconds to 1 minute at the most. They should be light golden brown when removed. Overcooking will toughen the squid.

To make about 60

Batter
½ cup cornstarch
½ cup all purpose flour
½ teaspoon baking
   soda
¼ teaspoon salt
1 egg, lightly beaten
2 teaspoons rice
   vinegar
2 tablespoons oil
½ cup water (more if
   needed)

1 pound small squid (5-
   inch body)
Oil for deep frying

JADE BALLS

Burma

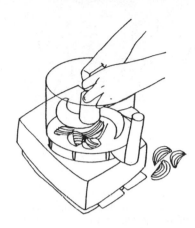

1. Soak peas overnight. Make sure that the peas are covered by at least one inch of water. Purée onion and chili in a blender or food processor.

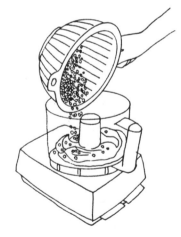

2. Drain peas and add them to the mixture together with coriander, turmeric, and salt. Process until a smooth mixture is produced.

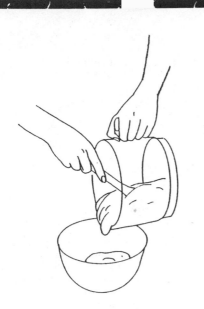

Makes about 150

1 cup split peas (soaked
   in water overnight)
1 large onion, chopped
1 fresh chili, chopped
½ teaspoon ground
   coriander
½ teaspoon ground
   turmeric
½ teaspoon salt
Oil for deep frying

5. During the last few seconds of frying time turn the balls over with a strainer about 10 times. The end result should be golden brown on one side and bright green on the other. Remove them with a strainer and drain on several layers of paper towel.

3. Transfer to a small bowl to prepare for frying. Heat oil in a wok or deep fryer to 320° F.

4. Drop teaspoonfuls of the mixture into the hot oil. Cook about 15 at a time. Fry them undisturbed for about 2 minutes.

LUMPIA

Philippines

1. Heat chicken stock in a medium-size saucepan and add chicken breast, pork, and bay leaf. Cover and cook over low heat for 15 to 20 minutes. Remove chicken and pork, and discard bay leaf. Set pan of stock aside. Begin soaking dried shrimp while chicken and pork is being cooked.

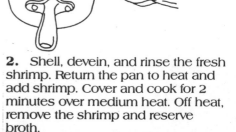

2. Shell, devein, and rinse the fresh shrimp. Return the pan to heat and add shrimp. Cover and cook for 2 minutes over medium heat. Off heat, remove the shrimp and reserve broth.

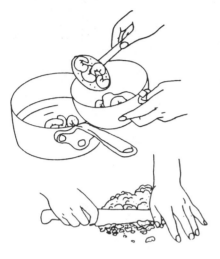

3. When chicken, pork, and fresh shrimp are cool enough to handle, chop them fine and set aside. Mince dried shrimp.

5. Add chopped chicken, pork, and fresh shrimp and stir fry for 2 minutes. Add ¼ cup of reserved broth and soy sauce and stir fry for another 2 minutes.

4. Heat lard in a skillet over medium heat and add garlic and scallions. Cook for 5 minutes, stirring constantly so that they do not brown. Add minced dried shrimp. Add green beans, Chinese cabbage, and bean sprouts. Stir fry for a minute after each addition.

6. Remove the entire contents of the skillet to a colander set over a bowl and drain for 30 minutes. Reserve the liquid for the dipping sauce.

To make 48

1½ cups chicken stock
1 whole chicken breast, boned and skinned
¼ pound lean pork
½ bay leaf
2 tablespoons dried shrimp (available in Oriental markets), soaked in ½ cup tepid water for 30 minutes and minced
6 ounces fresh shrimp, shelled and deveined
2 tablespoons lard
1 clove garlic, minced
½ cup minced scallions
10 green beans, cut in thin diagonal slices
3 cups finely chopped Chinese cabbage
2 cups bean sprouts, washed and stringy root tip pinched off
2 teaspoons soy sauce
1 egg white, lightly beaten
24 spring roll wrappers (See Ingredients, page xiii)
Oil for deep frying

Dipping Sauce
Reserved liquid drained from filling, plus enough chicken stock to make 1 cup
¼ cup light soy sauce
¼ cup brown sugar
1 clove garlic, crushed
2 tablespoons cornstarch
¼ cup water

21

LUMPIA

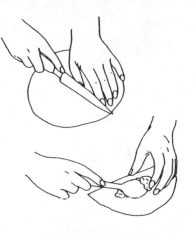

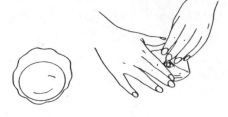

7. Beat egg white. Cut each spring roll wrapper in half. Place the straight edge toward you. Put a heaping teaspoon of filling at the one-third point.

9. Using your finger, wet the curved edge with egg white. Fold over and seal. The filling should be completely enclosed. The end product is a neat cylinder shape.

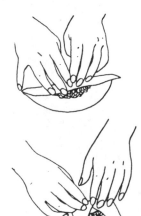

8. Cover the filling with the straight edge. Fold left and right sides over.

10. You may prepare the lumpia to this point up to 2 hours before frying. Cover with plastic wrap and refrigerate.

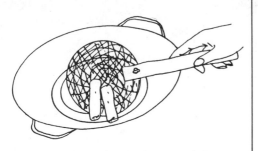

11. Pour 1 inch of oil into a skillet or wok and heat to 375° F. Fry the lumpia for 2 minutes, or until golden brown. Drain on paper towels. Serve with dipping sauce.

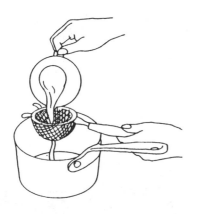

12. To make the dipping sauce, measure the reserved liquid, add chicken stock to make 1 cup, and strain into a small saucepan. Add soy sauce, brown sugar, and garlic. Bring to a boil and cook for 5 minutes. Remove garlic and discard. Moisten the cornstarch with water and stir into the sauce. Simmer while stirring until the mixture thickens.

ONION FRITTERS

India

TECHNIQUES
When you finish cutting hot chilies be sure to wash your hands, the cutting board, and knife with soap and water. Oil from a hot chili can irritate the skin and easily get into the eyes. In Step 10, don't fry more than 4 or 5 fritters at once. If you do, the oil temperature will be lowered and greasy fritters will result.

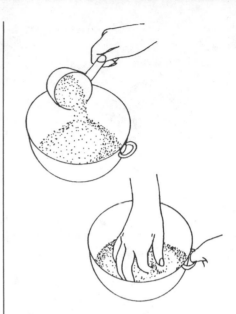

1. Put chickpea flour in a mixing bowl. Add peanut oil and mix thoroughly until there are no lumps.

2. Rinse the chili under running water. Cut the stem off.

3. Cut the pod in half, lengthwise. Scrape off the seeds.

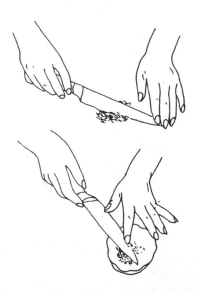

4. Mince the chili and set aside.

5. Mince the scallion.

6. Add cumin, salt, scallion, and chili to the chickpea flour.

ONION FRITTERS

7. With an electric mixer, gradually beat in the water. Mix for about 10 minutes or until the batter is smooth. Cover with plastic wrap and set aside for one hour.

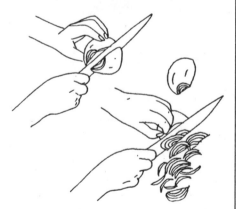

8. Cut onions as shown. Slice.

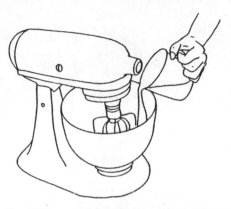

9. Add onions to the batter and mix until the onions are thoroughly coated. Let stand 10 minutes at room temperature.

10. Heat oil in a wok or deep fryer to 350° F. Drop 4 or 5 tablespoons of coated onions into hot oil. Fry for about 5 or 6 minutes until they are crisp and golden brown.

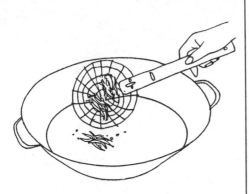

11. Remove with a strainer and drain on paper towels. Fritters may be fried ahead of time and refried for one minute in hot oil or warmed for two minutes on a cookie sheet in a 400° F. oven. Serve warm.

PEANUT WAFERS

Indonesia

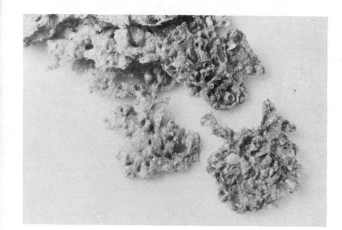

1. Sift rice flour, curry powder, and salt into a bowl. With a mortar and pestle grind rice to a rough cornmeal texture. Add ground rice and onion to flour mixture.

2. Gradually add coconut milk. Beat to a smooth batter, about the consistency of pancake batter.

TECHNIQUES
The recipe for preparing Coconut Milk appears on page 132, if you want to make your own.

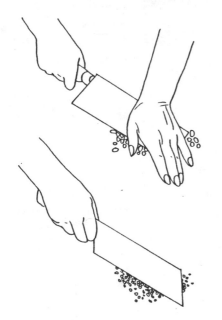

3. Chop the peanuts and stir them into the mixture.

4. Heat about ½ inch of oil in a large frying pan over medium heat.

5. Drop a few tablespoons of batter into the oil. The batter should spread to a thin lacelike wafer. If it doesn't, thin further with coconut milk. Fry until the underside turns golden brown.

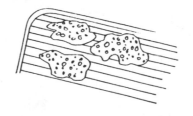

6. Turn wafers and continue frying to golden brown on the other side. Remove and drain on a wire rack.

½ cup rice flour
1 teaspoon curry
    powder
¾ teaspoon salt
2 tablespoons raw rice
1 tablespoon
    dehydrated, minced
    onion
14-ounce can coconut
    milk
¾ cup roasted,
    unsalted peanuts,
    chopped
Oil for deep frying

SAMOOSA

India

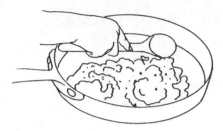

1. Heat oil in a skillet over medium heat. Add ginger, garlic, and scallions. Sauté until scallions are soft. Add curry powder, salt, and lime juice. Mix well. Turn up heat and add beef. Mash with back of spoon to break up lumps. Cook until brown.

2. Turn heat down to medium and add stock or water. Cover and cook until all liquid has been absorbed. Stir frequently to prevent sticking. Remove from heat and stir in garam masala and coriander. When completely cool, mix in onion.

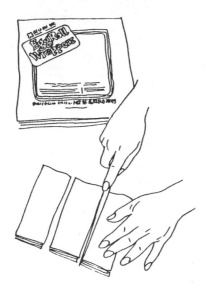

3. Cut egg roll wrappers into thirds.

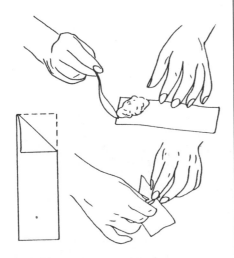

4. Put a teaspoon of filling on a corner and fold the strip over diagonally. Continue to fold diagonally.

5. Brush beaten egg on the last fold, and press tightly to seal. When all triangles are made, dip each into remaining beaten egg and roll in breadcrumbs.

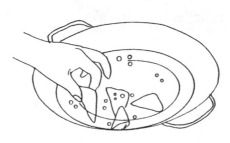

6. Heat oil in deep fryer or wok to 360° F. Add triangles a few at a time and fry until golden brown. Drain on a wire rack. Serve while hot. These go well with hot sauce.

To make 45

1 tablespoon oil
1 tablespoon fresh
    ginger, minced
1 clove garlic, minced
6 scallions, minced
    (about 1 cup)
2 tablespoons curry
    powder
½ teaspoon salt
1 tablespoon lime juice
8 ounces ground round
½ cup beef stock or
    water
3 tablespoons
    coriander, chopped
1 teaspoon garam
    masala
1 medium onion, finely
    minced
15 egg roll wrappers
1 egg beaten with 1
    tablespoon of water
1 cup breadcrumbs
Oil for deep frying

SEMOLINA PUFFS

India

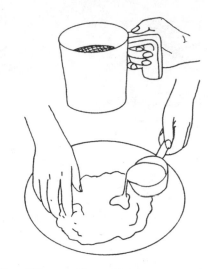

1. Sift semolina, all purpose and chickpea flours, salt, and curry powder together in a bowl. Pour in just enough water to make a lumpy dough. The dough should hold together when formed into a ball.

2. Turn the dough out onto a lightly floured board and knead for 10 minutes.

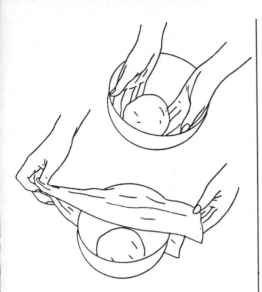

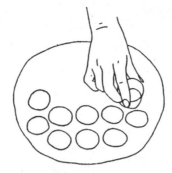

5. Using a 1¾-inch biscuit cutter, cut out as many rounds as you can. Place the disks on a cookie sheet and cover with a damp cloth to prevent them from drying out. Finish the other half of the dough in the same manner. Allow to rest for about 15 minutes.

3. Pat the dough into a small ball and put into a clean bowl. Cover with a damp cloth and let it set for 30 to 40 minutes.

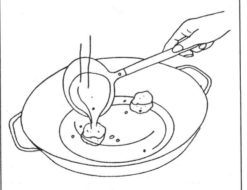

6. Heat the oil and the clarified butter (if you use it) in a wok to 375° F. The oil should be at least 2 inches deep. Drop 2 or 3 disks into the hot oil and, with a ladle, pour hot oil on them. This will cause them to puff up nicely. Remove the puffs and drain on a paper towel. You may prepare the puffs ahead up to this point. Just before serving, crisp them in a preheated 350° F. oven for 5 minutes.

4. Divide the dough in half and roll one half into a flat round about 16 inches in diameter by ⅟₁₆ inch thick.

To make about 36

½ cup semolina flour
½ cup all purpose flour
2 teaspoons chickpea
   flour
½ teaspoon salt
1 teaspoon curry
   powder
7 tablespoons water
   (more if necessary)
Vegetable oil for deep
   frying
¼ cup clarified butter
   (optional)

SESAME SEED CHICKEN

Japan

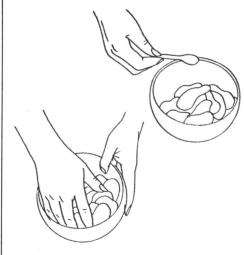

1. Skin and bone the whole chicken breast. Slice breast halves in thin (¼ inch) slanted slices.

2. Sprinkle the chicken slices with salt, sake, and lemon juice. Mix well and set aside.

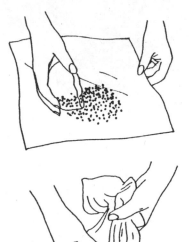

3. To cleanse sesame seeds, wrap with a damp cloth and lightly knead with the fingers.

4. Beat egg white lightly with a fork. Dust a slice of chicken with flour and dip into egg white. Coat evenly with sesame seeds and set aside.

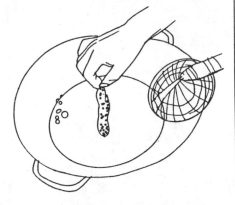

5. Heat oil in a frying pan to 350° F. Fry chicken pieces, a few at a time, for 1 minute. Turn and fry for another minute on the other side. Remove and drain on a wire rack.

To make about 20

1 whole chicken breast
¾ tablespoon salt
½ tablespoon sake
1 tablespoon lemon
   juice
4 tablespoons white
   sesame seeds
1 egg white
Flour
Oil for deep frying

SESAME
SHRIMP BALLS

China

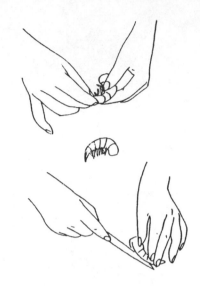

1. Shell and devein shrimp. Put them in a bowl with 1 teaspoon salt and mix gently with fingers. Rinse with several changes of water. Drain.

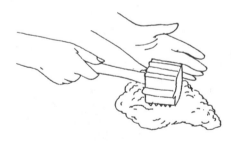

2. Using the back of a cleaver or a meat tenderizing mallet, pound the shrimp into a fine mash. Place in a bowl. Mince the water chestnuts fine. Add to the shrimp paste along with the rest of the shrimp paste ingredients. Mix thoroughly. Cover with plastic wrap and refrigerate for 2 hours.

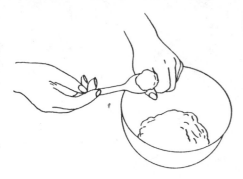

3. Heat 4 inches of water in a large saucepan. When the water comes to a boil turn the heat down to medium. Take some shrimp paste in the left hand. Squeeze a bit through the opening between the thumb and base of forefinger as shown. Scoop up the paste with a wet teaspoon.

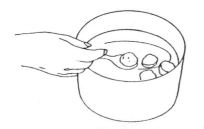

4. Gently drop the paste ball into the boiling water. The ball will sink. When it is cooked it will float to the surface. This takes about 5 minutes. You can test the doneness by squeezing it between the index finger and thumb. It should feel spongy. When done remove with a strainer.

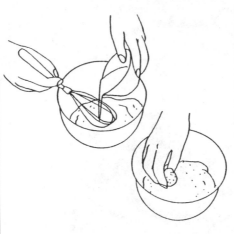

5. Heat oil in a wok to 350° F. Put ½ cup flour in a large bowl and beat in egg white and water. Coat shrimp balls with mixture, using just enough to act as a paste for sesame seeds.

6. Roll the coated balls in sesame seeds. Drop them into moderately hot oil and fry until golden brown—about 30 seconds.

To make about 40

Shrimp Paste
1 pound fresh shrimp
1 teaspoon salt
1 can water chestnuts, drained
3 egg whites, lightly beaten
¾ teaspoon salt
½ teaspoon sesame seed oil
1 scallion, white part only, minced
1 teaspoon fresh ginger juice
1 tablespoon dry sherry
3 tablespoons all purpose flour

Batter
½ cup all purpose flour
1 egg white
½ cup water
1 cup white sesame seeds

37

SHRIMP TOAST

China

1. Shell and devein 24 medium-size shrimp. Leave the tails on one dozen. Slice those with tails almost in half lengthwise so that the shrimp may be opened and flattened out.

2. Wash gently, stirring well. Rinse and drain several times. Pat dry with a paper towel.

3. Mince those shrimp without tails into fine pieces. An oriental chef's knife is excellent for this.

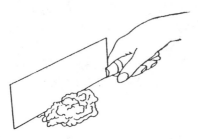

4. Using the back of the knife, chop into a fine mash. A knife rather than a food processor should be used. You want to retain some of the texture of the shrimp.

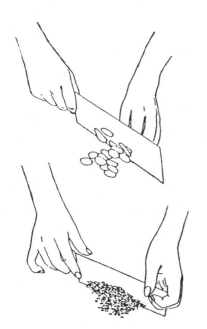

5. Mince the water chestnuts.

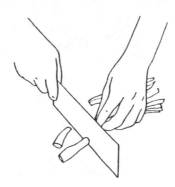

6. Mince the white sections of scallions.

7. Break off a small piece of fresh ginger root and peel. Mince. Do not use the powdered variety.

8. Place the minced shrimp in a mixing bowl and combine with other minced ingredients. Add flour, salt, sherry, and sesame seed oil.

To make 12

24 medium-size fresh shrimp (about ½ pound)
3 canned water chestnuts
2 scallions, white part only
⅓ teaspoon fresh minced ginger root
1 teaspoon flour
½ teaspoon salt
2 teaspoons dry sherry
1 teaspoon sesame seed oil
1 egg white
2 slices white bread
Oil for deep frying

SHRIMP TOAST

9. Add the white of one egg.

10. Thoroughly mix the ingredients by hand. Refrigerate for two hours to firm the mixture.

11. Cut 12 thin bread rectangles, about 1 × 2 inches.

12. Spread a little of the shrimp mixture on a bread wafer. This will tend to bind the whole shrimp to the bread.

13. Press an opened flat shrimp into the shrimp paste, cut side down. Spoon more shrimp paste onto the top.

14. Heat 4 inches of oil in a wok to 350° F. Place shrimp wafers in oil, shrimp side down. Deep fry for 1½ minutes. Turn over and fry, bread side down, for 10 seconds. Drain on paper towel. Serve hot.

SWEET AND SOUR PORK BALLS

China

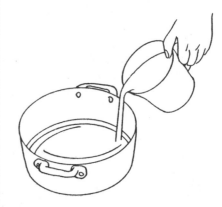

1. Mix pork ball ingredients together in a bowl. Stir well in one direction. Place in the refrigerator for one hour.

2. After the pork ball mixture has been chilled, heat chicken stock or water in a large skillet.

3. Scoop up some of the mixture in the left hand. Squeeze a ball of it through the hollow between the thumb and base of the index finger. Moisten a teaspoon in cold water. The spoon can be used to shape the ball a little better, and then to lift it off.

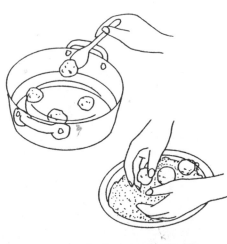

4. Drop the balls into the boiling chicken stock. Poach for 7 minutes and remove with a strainer. Dust with cornstarch while warm. Cool to room temperature before frying.

5. Sweet and sour sauce can be made while pork balls are cooling. Heat salt, sugar, water, vinegar, and tomato paste in a saucepan. Stir well to dissolve sugar. When the liquid comes to a boil, add cornstarch/stock mixture while stirring constantly until thick. Keep warm.

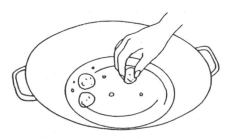

6. Heat oil in wok to 350° F. and deep fry the dusted balls for 3 minutes or until golden brown. Serve with sweet and sour sauce as a dip.

To make 40

Pork Ball Mixture
1 pound ground pork
1 teaspoon finely
    minced fresh ginger
    root
1 scallion, minced
2 whole eggs
1 tablespoon dry sherry
¼ teaspoon white
    pepper
½ teaspoon salt
½ teaspoon sesame
    seed oil
2 tablespoons
    cornstarch
1 tablespoon water
1 quart chicken stock or
    water
½ cup cornstarch

Sweet and Sour Sauce
¼ teaspoon salt
1 cup sugar
½ cup water
½ cup rice vinegar
1 tablespoon tomato
    paste
3 tablespoons
    cornstarch mixed
    with 3 tablespoons
    chicken stock

Oil for deep frying

PAN FRIED

CHINESE PIZZA

China

1. Measure flour into a large bowl. Boil water and immediately pour onto flour. Stir with a wooden spatula or chopsticks until cool enough to handle.

2. Sprinkle pastry board lightly with flour and knead until smooth and elastic, about 10 minutes. This can be done with a mixer or food processor if available.

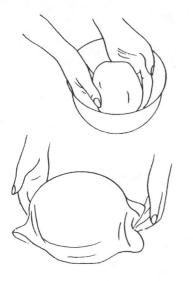

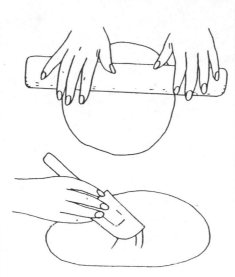

Dough
2 cups all purpose flour
1 cup boiling water

2 tablespoons lard, softened
½ teaspoon salt (omit if anchovies are used)
1 cup minced scallion
1 cup julienned uncooked bacon
8 fillets of anchovies, minced (optional)

Oil

3. Form the dough into a smooth ball and place in a clean bowl. Cover with a damp cloth. Let dough rest for 35 to 45 minutes.

5. Roll one portion into a circular sheet about 10 inches in diameter. Spread ½ tablespoon of lard evenly onto the dough.

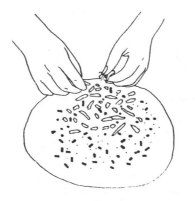

4. Divide the dough into four portions and knead each for about a minute on a lightly floured board.

6. If no anchovies are to be used, sprinkle ¼ of the salt over the surface. Evenly distribute ¼ of scallions, bacon, and anchovies.

CHINESE PIZZA

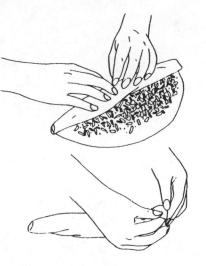

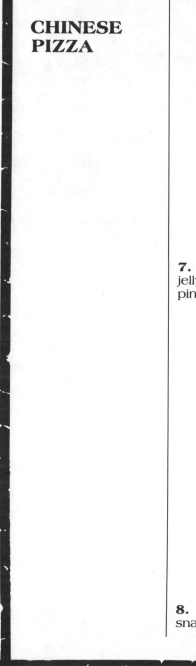

7. Roll up the dough tightly, like a jelly roll, and seal each end by pinching.

8. Twirl the dough around like a snail, Danish pastry style.

9. Flatten gently with the palm of your hand. On a lightly floured board, gently roll dough out to about 8 inches in diameter. Be careful not to rupture it. Prepare the rest of the dough in the same manner.

10. Heat enough oil to cover ¼ inch of the bottom of the frying pan. Slip a pizza into the hot oil. Turn the heat down to low and fry for 8 to 10 minutes. Flip and fry for another 8 to 10 minutes until golden brown on both sides.

11. Take pizza out to drain on paper towels. Cut into 8 wedge-shaped pieces. Serve hot.

CURRIED SHIITAKE

Japan

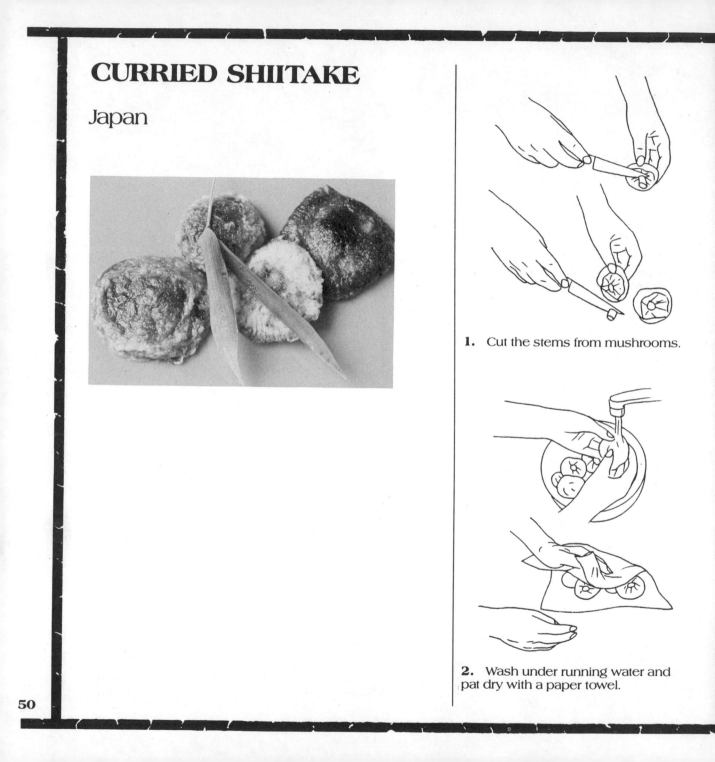

1. Cut the stems from mushrooms.

2. Wash under running water and pat dry with a paper towel.

3. Sprinkle salt on both sides of the mushroom caps.

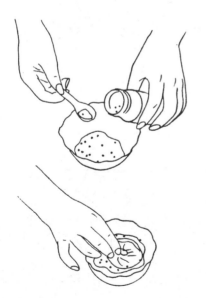

4. Mix flour and curry powder and dust mushrooms.

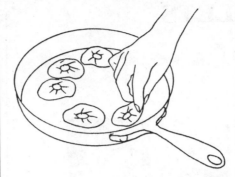

5. Heat oil in a frying pan. Add the mushroom caps and cook until just done (about 2 minutes on each side). Serve hot.

8 fresh shiitake
   mushrooms
Salt
2½ tablespoons flour
½ teaspoon curry
   powder
1½ tablespoons oil

FISH OMELETS

Thailand

TECHNIQUES
Lard imparts a wonderful flavor to these omelets, but a vegetable oil may be substituted for health reasons, if necessary.

1. Flake the tuna into a bowl.

2. Beat eggs well and mix in with tuna.

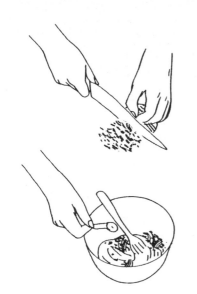

3. Mince onion and chop coriander. Add to egg mixture. Add salt and pepper. Mix well.

4. Heat lard in a large skillet. Pour 2 tablespoons of the egg mixture per omelet into the pan. Spread with the back of the spoon to make a thin round omelet about 2 to 3 inches in diameter.

5. Cook the omelet until set. Flip and cook the other side. Remove with a spatula. Repeat with the remaining egg mixture. Omelets may be prepared ahead and reheated by laying them separately on a cookie sheet and placing in a preheated 400° F. oven.

To make 36

½ cup water-packed tuna, drained
5 eggs
½ cup minced onion
4 to 5 sprigs coriander, chopped
¼ teaspoon salt
¼ teaspoon pepper
1 tablespoon lard

MARINATED CHICKEN LIVERS

Japan

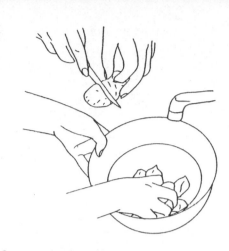

1. Cut each chicken liver in half. Add 1 tablespoon of salt to a bowl of water. Soak the livers, squeezing them gently a few times to remove blood. Rinse well and drain.

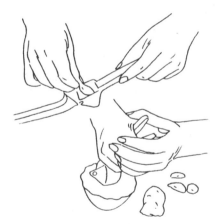

TECHNIQUES
Care should be taken not to overcook the livers. Try to leave them a little pink. Liver rapidly becomes dry when overcooked.

2. To make the marinade, break off a piece of fresh ginger about 2 inches long. Peel and cut into small pieces. Using a garlic press, squeeze 1½ tablespoons of juice into a bowl.

3. Add sake. Pour over livers and mix well. Allow to marinate for 15 minutes.

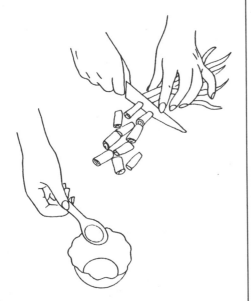

4. Cut scallions into 1 inch lengths. In a small bowl, mix together soy sauce, mirin, and sugar. Set aside.

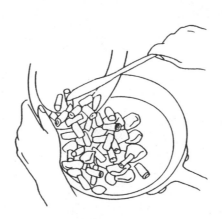

5. Heat 3 tablespoons of oil in a skillet over high heat and brown livers quickly. Add scallions and sauté for one minute. Pour in soy sauce, mirin, and sugar mixture and cook for another minute.

6. Remove from heat. Pierce each liver piece with a toothpick, add a scallion piece, and serve hot.

To serve 8

1 pound chicken livers
1 tablespoon salt

Marinade
1½ tablespoons fresh
 ginger juice
1½ tablespoons sake
1 bunch large scallions
3 tablespoons soy
 sauce
1½ tablespoons mirin
3 tablespoons sugar

3 tablespoons oil
Toothpicks

POT STICKERS

China

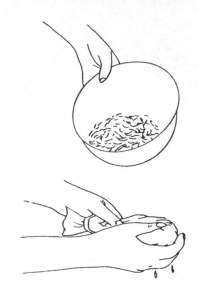

1. To make the filling, place chopped Chinese cabbage in a bowl and sprinkle with salt. Mix and set aside for 10 minutes. Place it in a towel and squeeze out the moisture.

2. Combine the pork and salted water in a bowl. Mix well in a circular motion for a couple of minutes.

TECHNIQUES
Pay particular attention to Step 9. It is especially important that the pot stickers stand upright with the pinched edge upward. This will allow uniform cooking of each, and will permit a nicer presentation.

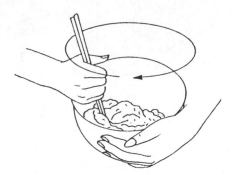

3. Add the cabbage and the rest of the filling ingredients. Again, mix with a circular motion until all of the ingredients are well blended. Chinese chefs all recommend mixing in one direction only. Cover and refrigerate for about an hour.

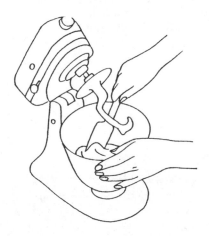

4. To make the dough, measure the flour into a large bowl. Gradually add water and mix until dough forms. Knead until smooth and elastic (about 5 minutes). A food processor or an electric mixer with dough hook should be used if available.

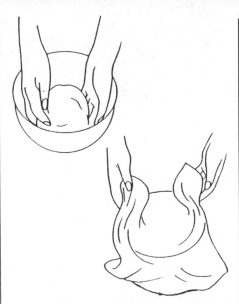

5. Pat the dough into a smooth ball and put in a clean bowl. Cover with a damp cloth and let it rest for 20 minutes.

6. Roll the dough into a long cylinder, about 1 inch in diameter. Cut into 1-inch-long pieces and roll each into a little ball.

To make 18 to 20

Filling
2 cups finely chopped Chinese cabbage
1 teaspoon salt
1 cup ground pork butt
3 tablespoons water with ½ teaspoon salt
1 cup raw shrimp, shelled, deveined, minced
1 egg, lightly beaten
1½ tablespoons soy sauce
1 tablespoon sesame seed oil

Dough
2 cups all purpose flour
¾ cup cold water

Cornstarch
Oil for cooking
Hot water

57

POT STICKERS

7. Sprinkle a ball of dough lightly with flour and flatten with the palm of your hand. With a small rolling pin, roll into a 3-inch circle slightly thicker at the center than the edge. Repeat with the rest of the balls. Cover the finished disks to prevent drying out.

9. Fold the disk in half, and starting from one end pinch the edge of the dough in an overlapping fashion, as shown. Place on a cookie sheet sprinkled with cornstarch. The dumplings should stand with the pinched edge upright.

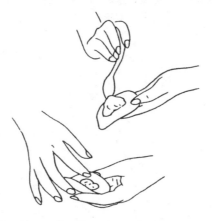

8. To make the dumplings, put a teaspoon of filling in the center of a disk. Wet the inside rim of the disk with a finger that has been dipped in water.

10. Heat a large, heavy frying pan over medium heat and add enough oil to coat the bottom of the pan. Off heat, arrange the dumplings in a row across the center of the pan, flat side down.

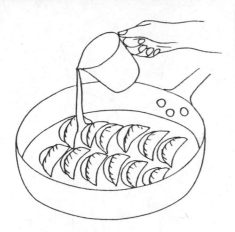

11. Return the pan to the heat and fry dumplings until the bottoms turn light brown. Add ¼ cup of hot water, cover, and cook over medium heat until the water evaporates, about 8 to 10 minutes.

12. Uncover and add 1 tablespoon of oil evenly around the dumplings. Fry until the bottoms become nicely brown and crisp. Serve with chili oil (page 130) and rice vinegar, which are mixed together according to taste in a small side dish by each person at the table. The pot sticker is dipped into this mixture before eating.

RANGOON SHRIMP

Burma

1. Shell and devein shrimp.

2. Put the shrimp in a bowl with salt and gently mix with fingers. Rinse with several changes of water and drain well.

3. Combine the marinade ingredients in a large bowl. Add shrimp. Mix thoroughly to coat the shrimp. Set aside for 30 minutes at room temperature.

4. Place 2 shrimp on each skewer.

5. Heat 2 tablespoons of peanut oil in a large skillet at high heat. Add the shrimp and cook, turning once, until just done, about 1 to 2 minutes on each side.

To make 16

32 fresh shrimp
1 teaspoon salt

Marinade
⅓ teaspoon salt
¼ teaspoon cayenne
    pepper
2 teaspoons turmeric
2 tablespoons lime
    juice
1 teaspoon sesame
    seed oil

2 tablespoons peanut
    oil
Short bamboo skewers

61

TAMARIND SHRIMP

Indonesia

1. Shell and devein shrimp, leaving last shell section and tail intact.

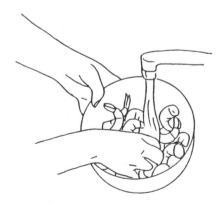

2. Place in a bowl with 1 teaspoon salt. Mix gently with fingers. Rinse with several changes of water and drain. Set aside.

3. Peel and press a clove of garlic into a large bowl.

4. Add ½ teaspoon salt, grated lime rind, tamarind water, sugar, pepper, and shrimp. Mix well to coat shrimp thoroughly. Marinate for 20 minutes at room temperature.

5. Heat butter in a large skillet. Add shrimp and cook while turning them occasionally for 3 to 4 minutes or until they are firm and pink.

6. Remove to a serving plate. Squeeze the juice of a lime over the shrimp and serve hot.

To make about 2½ dozen

1 pound shrimp
1 teaspoon salt

Marinade
1 clove garlic
½ teaspoon salt
1 teaspoon grated lime
    rind
¼ cup tamarind water
1 teaspoon sugar
¼ teaspoon pepper

2 tablespoons butter
1 lime

WALNUT CHICKEN

China

1. Skin and bone the chicken breast. Cut into two halves. Remove the fillets. Pull the tendons out.

2. Lay one half flat on the cutting board and slice in half horizontally. Do not cut all the way through.

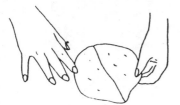

3. Open fillet and lay flat.

4. Score lightly with a cleaver or sharp knife.

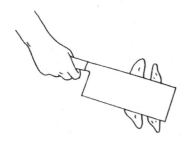

5. Flatten the two fillets with the side of your cleaver.

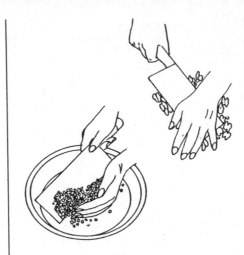

6. Crush and chop walnuts to about the size of peppercorns.

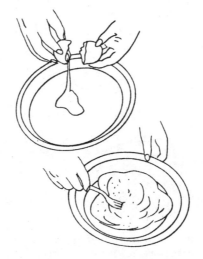

7. In a large shallow bowl place egg whites, sherry, pepper, sesame seed oil, salt, and water. Mix well and stir in the flour.

To make about 20

1 whole chicken breast
2 cups walnuts, coarsely chopped
2 egg whites
1 tablespoon dry sherry
¼ teaspoon white pepper
½ teaspoon sesame seed oil
¾ teaspoon salt
¼ cup water
½ cup all purpose flour
Oil

WALNUT CHICKEN

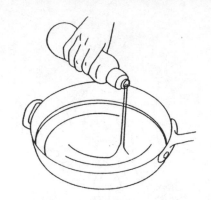

8. Set a large frying pan over moderately high heat. Add enough oil to coat the bottom of the pan to ⅛ inch. Heat to very hot but not smoking. Turn heat down to low.

9. Dip chicken pieces into the flour mixture, coating both sides, and then coat both sides well with walnuts.

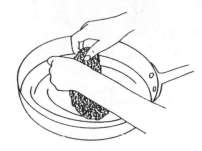

10. Brown very slowly. Patience is important. The walnuts will burn if cooked too rapidly. Browning should take about 5 minutes.

11. Turn to fry the other side. If needed, pour little droplets of oil around to keep things moist.

12. Slice in bite-size pieces and serve.

BARBECUED

BEEF SASHIMI

Japan

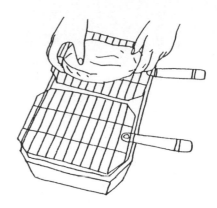

1. Start the barbecue and allow the coals to burn until white ash appears. Trim the fat and sinew from the fillet. Broil a couple of inches away from red hot charcoal until surface is browned all over. Do not overcook.

2. Plunge beef into ice water and wash off any burned pieces. Pat dry with paper towel and set aside.

TECHNIQUES
In Step 2, plunging the meat into ice water causes the meat to firm up.

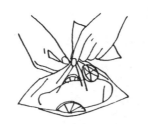

For 8 to 12 people

2-pound fillet of beef (in
    one piece)
Large bowl of ice water

Marinade
½ onion, sliced thin
2 cloves garlic, sliced
    thin
½ lemon, sliced thin
¾ cup rice vinegar
½ cup soy sauce
¼ cup sake

Large plastic bag

3. Thinly slice onion, garlic, and lemon. Combine rice vinegar, soy sauce, and sake.

5. Remove the air from the bag and tie it tightly. Place it in the refrigerator for 24 to 36 hours.

6. Remove the fillet from the marinade and slice it into thin 1- × 2-inch slices against the grain. Serve.

4. Place the fillet in a large plastic bag. Add all of the marinade ingredients to the bag.

BEEF SATAY

Indonesia

1. Soak skewers. If you will be using charcoal, light the coals. Combine marinade ingredients in a small saucepan and simmer for ten minutes. Set aside to cool.

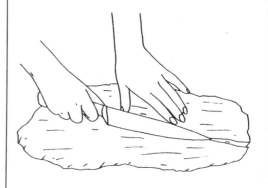

2. Cut the meat into 2-inch-wide strips with the grain.

TECHNIQUES
If you intend to use charcoal in Step 6, allow the coals to burn until they are covered with a white ash before starting to broil the meat.

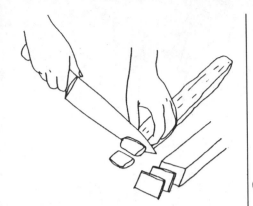

3. Holding the knife at a 20° angle, slice meat thinly against the grain. (Angle slicing tenderizes the meat.) You should have 60 slices.

5. Pour the marinade over the skewered meat. Turn each to make sure that the marinade fully coats all of them. Repeat turning several times during the marinade period. Marinate for 1 hour at room temperature or 2 hours in the refrigerator.

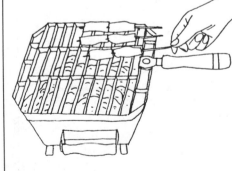

4. Thread two slices of meat on each skewer. Place them in a pan large enough so they lie flat.

6. Broil about 2 inches from a charcoal bed or a preheated oven broiler for about 8 to 10 minutes. Serve hot. Prepare sauce by combining all sauce ingredients in a pan and warming over low heat.

To make 30

30 bamboo skewers (soaked in water for one hour to prevent burning)

Marinade
1 tablespoon palm sugar
1 clove garlic, minced
¼ teaspoon salt
3 tablespoons soy sauce
¼ teaspoon ground coriander
¼ teaspoon minced ginger root
1 teaspoon ground cumin
1 tablespoon oil
⅓ cup water
1 pound flank steak

Satay Sauce
1 cup Crunchy Peanut Sauce (page 134)
2 tablespoons lime juice
1 tablespoon lime rind, grated
2 tablespoons tamarind juice
¼ cup beef stock or water

CHICKEN LOLLIPOPS

Indonesia

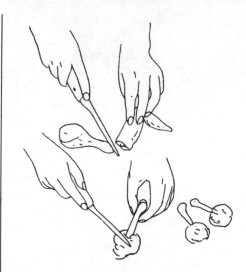

1. Cut the wings at the joint to separate the small drumstick. The remainder of the wing can go into your stockpot. Push the meat from the narrow end of the drumstick to the thick end. Place the drumsticks in a large bowl.

TECHNIQUES
In Step 5, the charcoal should be allowed to burn until it is covered with a white ash before you begin to cook.

2. Combine all of the ingredients for the marinade in a food processor or blender and process until the mixture is puréed.

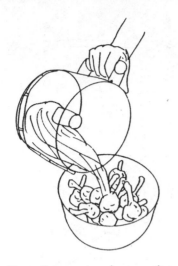

3. Pour the marinade over the drumsticks and let stand in the refrigerator overnight.

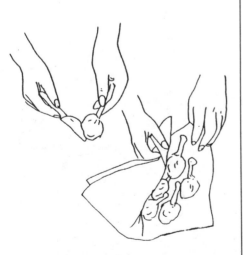

4. Scrape the marinade from the drumsticks and pat them dry with a paper towel. Reserve the marinade in a small saucepan.

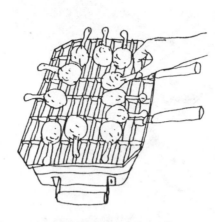

5. Light a barbecue or small hibachi and grill the drumsticks about 3 inches from the hot coals.

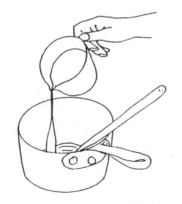

6. Heat the marinade. Add coconut milk and reduce the liquid to about 1 cup over medium low heat. Serve the chicken with sauce on the side as a dip. You may garnish the sauce with fresh coriander sprigs.

To make 32

32 chicken wings

Marinade
2 cloves garlic, peeled
1 small piece ginger root, peeled
1 onion, peeled and quartered
3 fresh chilies, seeded
2 teaspoons salt
1 teaspoon ground coriander seed
2 tablespoons soy sauce
3 tablespoons lime juice
2 tablespoons palm sugar
2 tablespoons oil

½ cup coconut milk
Fresh coriander sprigs (optional)

PINE CONE SQUID

Japan

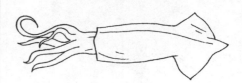

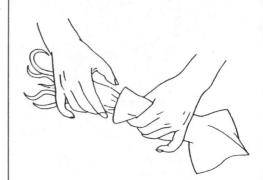

1. Gently pull the tentacles from the squid's body.

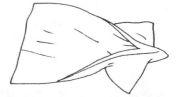

2. Cut the body open lengthwise.

TECHNIQUES

The diagonal undercutting shown in Step 6 will cause the cut edges to curl when broiled, thus creating an unusual surface texture. Do not overcook the squid. It will toughen very rapidly. It is done when the diagonal cuts begin to curl back and start to brown.

3. Cut the head (pointed part) off and discard.

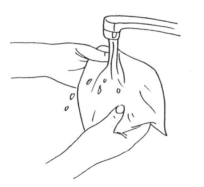

4. Rinse well under running water.

5. Lay the meat flat with the skin side up. Pull the skin off. If the skin is too slippery, a paper towel held between the finger and thumb will provide more friction.

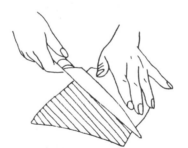

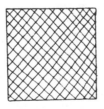

6. Score the meat diagonally as shown. The blade should be angled to undercut slightly.

To make 24

2 large squid (the sack part of the squid should be 8 or 9 inches long)
½ teaspoon ginger juice
2 tablespoons mirin
2 tablespoons soy sauce
4 long metal skewers

PINE CONE SQUID

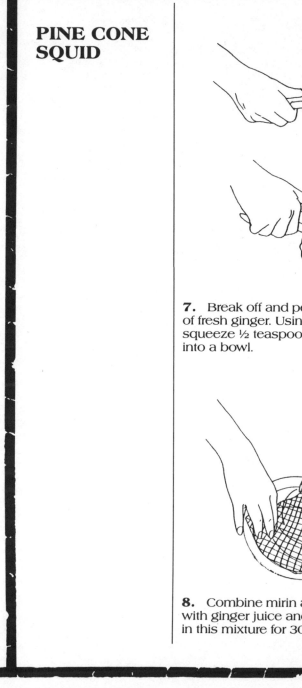

7. Break off and peel a small piece of fresh ginger. Using a garlic press, squeeze ½ teaspoon of ginger juice into a bowl.

8. Combine mirin and soy sauce with ginger juice and marinate squid in this mixture for 30 minutes.

9. Thread the metal skewers through the center of the squid meat as shown. Be careful that the skewers do not poke through the scored surface.

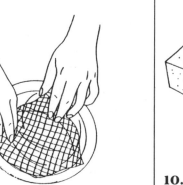

10. Broil for 2 minutes on each side. 2 bricks may be used for support. Brush the squid with marinade a couple of times. Do not overcook, or squid will toughen.

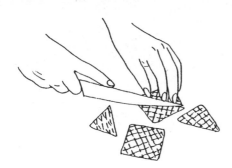

11. Remove skewers and cut the meat into triangles.

YAKITORI

Japan

TECHNIQUES

Bamboo skewers should be soaked in water for about 20 minutes prior to using. This will prevent the skewers from burning over the hot coals.

The coals should burn until they are covered with a white ash before you start to cook.

1. Light the charcoal. Soak the bamboo skewers in water for about 20 minutes. Combine soy sauce, sake, and mirin in a small saucepan and bring to a boil. Add sugar and juice of ginger. Reduce the mixture to ½ cup.

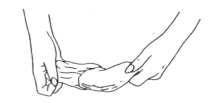

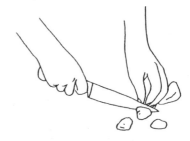

2. Skin and bone the legs and thighs. Cut each into nine pieces. The skin may be cut up and added if you like.

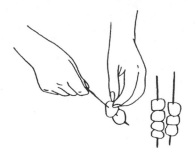

3. Thread 3 or 4 pieces of meat onto each skewer.

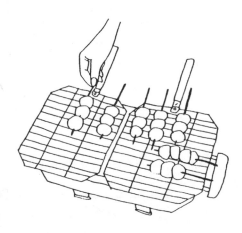

4. When the coals are ready (covered with a white ash) grill the skewered chicken about 2 or 3 inches from them for about 2 minutes. Turn and brush the sauce on the cooked side. Grill for 2 minutes on the other side. Turn and brush the sauce on again. Grill for 1 minute.

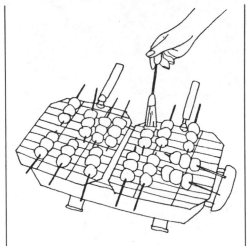

5. Continue to brush sauce on and grill sides at 1-minute intervals. Entire cooking time should not exceed 5 or 6 minutes. Brush the sauce on all over and serve while hot. Sprinkle sansho (pepper) powder on if you like.

To make 24

Charcoal
24 short bamboo
  skewers
6 tablespoons soy
  sauce
2 tablespoons sake
2 tablespoons mirin
6 tablespoons sugar
½ teaspoon ginger juice
4 chicken legs and
  thighs
Sansho powder
  (optional)

CHICKEN CRISPS p. 2

CHICKEN NORIMAKI p. 4

CHICKEN TATTA AGE p. 6

CRAB AND TOFU BALLS p. 8

FIVE SPICE SPARERIBS p. 10

FRIED CHICKEN WINGS p. 12

FRIED FISHCAKE p. 14

FRIED SQUID RINGS p. 16

JADE BALLS p. 18

LUMPIA p. 20

ONION FRITTERS p. 24

PEANUT WAFERS p. 28

SAMOOSA p. 30

SEMOLINA PUFFS p. 32

SESAME SEED CHICKEN p. 34

SESAME SHRIMP BALLS p. 36

SHRIMP TOAST p. 38

SWEET AND SOUR PORK BALLS p. 42

CHINESE PIZZA p. 46

CURRIED SHIITAKE p. 50

FISH OMELETS p. 52

MARINATED CHICKEN LIVERS p. 54

POT STICKERS p. 56

RANGOON SHRIMP p. 60

TAMARIND SHRIMP p. 62

WALNUT CHICKEN p. 64

BEEF SASHIMI p. 70

BEEF SATAY p. 72

CHICKEN LOLLIPOPS p. 74

PINE CONE SQUID p. 76

YAKITORI p. 80

EGG-ROLLED CRAB AND CHICKEN p. 84

FUN GOR p. 86

HAR GOW p. 88

SHIU MAI p. 90

SPICY STEAMED MUSSELS p. 92

STEAMED DUMPLINGS p. 94

STUFFED BLACK MUSHROOMS p. 98

CHICKEN LOAF p. 102

CURRIED CASHEW NUTS p. 104

GLAZED SPARERIBS p. 106

OVEN-BROILED OYSTERS p. 108

BROCCOLI WITH SOY DIP p. 112

CHICKEN IN LETTUCE CUPS p. 114

CUCUMBER WITH CRAB p. 118

CUCUMBER WITH WALNUT MISO p. 120

ROLLED SASHIMI p. 122

SEVICHE p. 124

EGG-ROLLED CRAB AND CHICKEN

Japan

TECHNIQUES
In the sketch for Step 5 we are using a square, stainless steel steamer rather than the conventional Chinese bamboo steamer. Both are excellent, but we find the square shape utilizes space more efficiently.

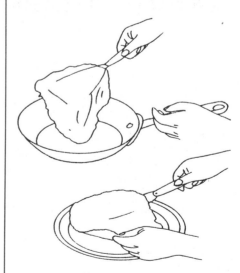

1. Lightly beat eggs in a bowl—just enough to break up the egg whites. Heat an 8-inch skillet over low heat and grease lightly with oil. Pour a third of the beaten eggs into the skillet and slant rapidly in all directions so the egg runs over the entire surface.

2. Carefully remove the egg skin from the skillet and lay it on a plate. Do the same twice more with the remaining eggs. Set aside.

STEAMED

3. Shred crabmeat by hand into a bowl. Bone and mince chicken breast and add to the crabmeat. Add the remaining ingredients. Mix well to blend and divide into three portions.

5. Put water in a steamer. Put a layer of cheesecloth in the upper portion. When the water comes to a boil, lay the omelet rolls in and steam, covered, for 25 to 30 minutes.

To make 24

3 eggs
Oil
8 ounces cooked
    crabmeat
1 whole chicken breast,
    boned and minced
    (about 12 ounces)
1 tablespoon minced
    scallion (green part
    only)
1 tablespoon sake
1 tablespoon light soy
    sauce
1 tablespoon
    cornstarch
½ teaspoon salt
2 tablespoons water

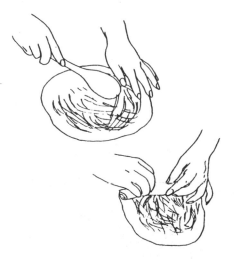

4. Place one of the portions on an egg skin and spread evenly. Roll it up jelly roll style, taking care not to rupture the egg skin. Prepare the other two rolls in the same manner.

6. Slice each roll into 1-inch pieces. Serve either hot or at room temperature.

FUN GOR

China

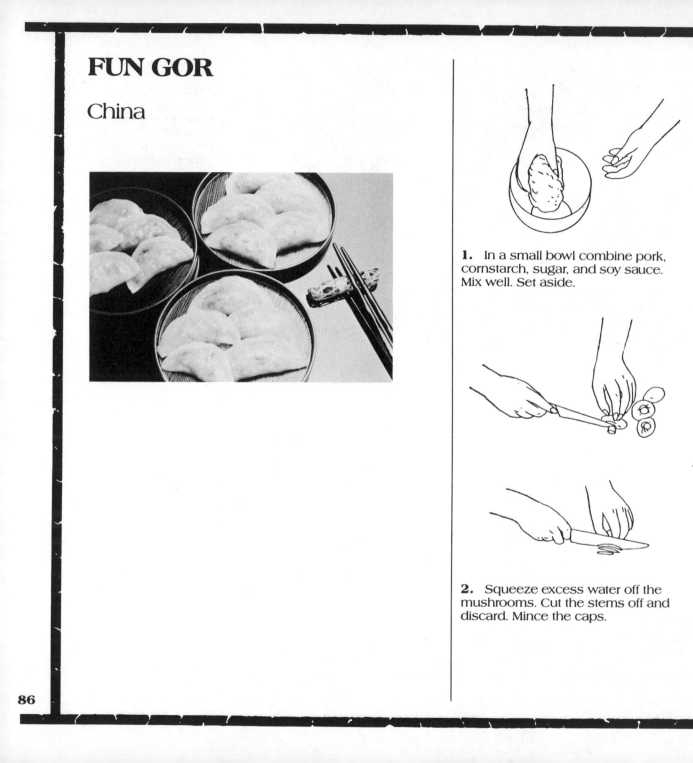

1. In a small bowl combine pork, cornstarch, sugar, and soy sauce. Mix well. Set aside.

2. Squeeze excess water off the mushrooms. Cut the stems off and discard. Mince the caps.

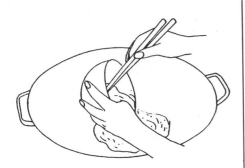

3. Heat 1 tablespoon of oil in a wok and stir fry pork mixture until cooked, about 5 minutes. Add mushrooms, water chestnuts and bamboo shoots. Stir fry for 2 more minutes.

4. Sprinkle in sherry and add scallion. Toss for a minute. Then pour in the cornstarch/water mixture. Stir fry until the filling thickens, 1 to 2 minutes. Transfer to bowl to cool.

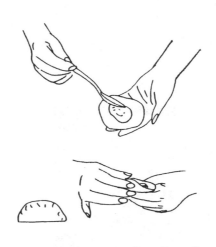

5. Make Fun Gor/Har Gow Dough (page 140). Place a heaping teaspoon of filling at the center of a dough disk. Fold and pinch the edges to seal. Place on a large oiled plate.

6. Heat water in the bottom section of your steamer. Oil the bottom of the steaming compartment. Place the Fun Gor in the steamer on their sides. Do not overlap. Steam, covered, for 5 minutes.

To make about 48

Filling
½ pound ground pork
2 teaspoons cornstarch
1 teaspoon sugar
2 teaspoons soy sauce
10 dried black
   mushrooms soaked
   in water to cover until
   reconstituted, tough
   stems removed, and
   minced, to make ½
   cup
Oil
⅓ cup minced water
   chestnuts
½ cup minced bamboo
   shoots
1 tablespoon sherry
2 scallions, white part
   only, minced
2 teaspoons cornstarch
   mixed with 1
   tablespoon water

Fun Gor/Har Gow
   Dough (page 140)
Oil

HAR GOW

China

1. Shell and devein shrimp. Put them in a bowl with 1 teaspoon of salt and gently mix with fingers. Rinse with several changes of water and drain well. Chop coarsely.

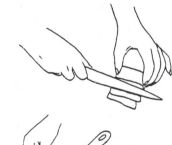

2. Blanch the salt pork by cutting into thin slices and dropping into 2 cups of simmering water for 8 minutes. Mince.

Filling

1 pound shrimp,
   shelled, deveined,
   and chopped
   coarsely
1 teaspoon salt (for
   cleaning shrimp)
¼ cup minced,
   blanched salt pork
6 water chestnuts,
   minced
1 scallion, white part
   only, minced
½ teaspoon sugar
1 tablespoon dry sherry
1 tablespoon
   cornstarch
½ tablespoon light soy
   sauce
½ teaspoon salt
2 teaspoons peanut oil
1 teaspoon sesame
   seed oil

Fun Gor/Har Gow
   Dough (page 140)
Oil

3. Mince water chestnuts and scallion. Combine all of the filling ingredients in a large bowl and stir in one direction until thoroughly mixed. Cover and refrigerate for 2 hours.

5. Place a heaping teaspoon of filling at the center of a dough wrapper. Bring the edges together and seal in a pleating fashion, as shown. Be sure to form a flat bottom. Place on the oiled plate. Repeat until all of the filling is used up.

6. Put your steamer on to boil. Oil the base of the steamer section. Place the Har Gow neatly in the steamer with space between each. Cover and steam for 5 minutes.

4. Prepare the Fun Gor/Har Gow Dough (page 140). Lightly oil a large plate.

89

SHIU MAI

China

TECHNIQUES
Chinese chefs will place the heel of the palm on top of a stack of wonton wrappers and fan them out like a deck of cards with a clockwise twisting motion. Try it. It makes them easier to pick up.

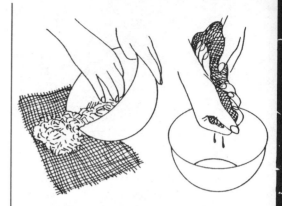

1. Chop the Chinese cabbage and place in a bowl. Sprinkle with salt. Pack cabbage down and let stand for 15 minutes. Empty into cheesecloth and squeeze out excess water. Set aside.

2. Mince scallion, coriander, and ginger root. Combine in a bowl with ground pork, soy sauce, sugar, sherry, cornstarch, sesame seed oil, and oyster sauce. Mix well. Thoroughly mix in the reserved cabbage. Refrigerate for about 20 minutes.

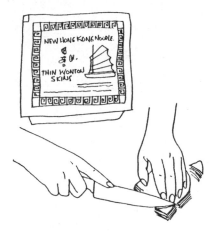

3. Oil a large plate. Remove the wonton wrappers from their package. Cut off the corners so they are circular in shape. Cover with a damp cloth.

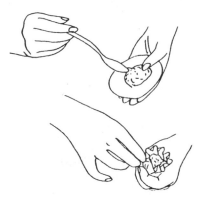

4. Take a wrapper. Place a tablespoon of filling in the center. Bring up the sides, allowing the folds to gather neatly. The gathered folds should be pressed lightly into the moist filling to adhere. The filling should be about ¼ from the top of the wrapper—not completely full, in other words. Top with a fresh pea.

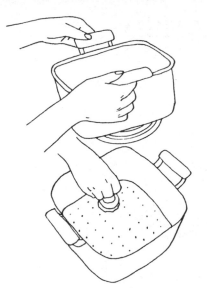

5. Boil water in the lower section of your steamer. Oil the base of the upper section.

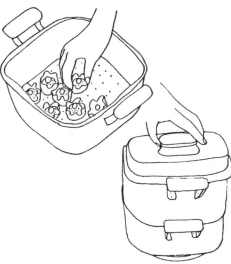

6. Place the Shiu Mai in the steamer, cover, and steam for 15 minutes. Serve hot.

To make about 36

Filling
1½ cups finely chopped Chinese cabbage
1 teaspoon salt
¼ cup minced scallion
¼ cup minced fresh coriander
½ cup finely minced fresh ginger root
1 pound ground pork butt
1½ tablespoons soy sauce
½ teaspoon sugar
2 tablespoons dry sherry
1 tablespoon cornstarch
1 teaspoon sesame seed oil
1 tablespoon oyster sauce

1 package wonton wrappers
Fresh peas
Water
Oil

SPICY STEAMED MUSSELS

India

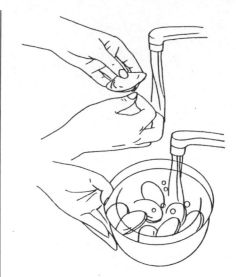

1. Scrub each mussel under running water and remove beard. Cover with cold water for a couple of hours to remove sand.

2. Heat oil in a saucepan over medium heat and fry onion, ginger, and garlic together until the onion is soft. Stir in chili, turmeric, ground coriander and salt. Cook slowly for about 10 minutes while stirring occasionally.

3. Remove from the heat and add lemon juice and fresh coriander. Stir well to blend. Set aside.

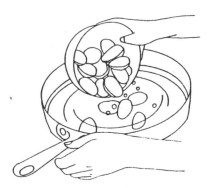

4. Cover the bottom of a large saucepan with ½ inch of water and wine mixture in equal parts. Add a pinch of baking soda. Drain mussels and add. Cover the pan and steam the mussels for 5 minutes or until shells open.

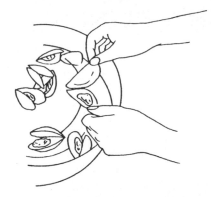

5. Discard any unopened mussels. Break off and discard the empty half of the shell. Loosen the mussel from the shell.

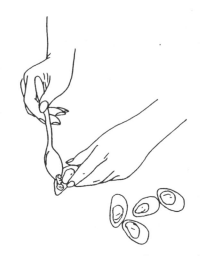

6. Spoon sauce on each mussel and serve.

Serves 8

1 pound mussels
2 tablespoons oil
1 large onion, finely
    chopped
2 teaspoons minced
    fresh ginger
1 large clove garlic,
    minced
1 teaspoon crushed
    chili
¼ teaspoon turmeric
1 teaspoon ground
    coriander
½ teaspoon salt
1 tablespoon lemon
    juice
2 sprigs fresh
    coriander, minced
Water
White wine
Pinch baking soda

STEAMED DUMPLINGS

Thailand

1. Sift the cake flour and corn flour together until they are well mixed.

2. Gradually add boiling water, stirring constantly.

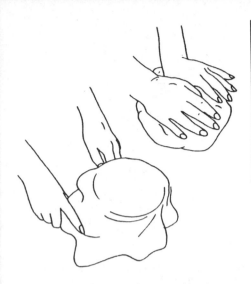

3. Knead into a smooth dough. Set aside in a bowl and cover with a damp cloth.

4. Heat oil in a skillet over medium heat. Sauté the onion until transparent. Add the pork. Mash with wooden spoon to break up lumps. Turn the meat constantly while cooking. Cook until all of the meat turns white. Add salt, pepper, and sugar.

5. Stir in peanuts and remove from heat.

6. With a perforated spoon remove as much fat as possible while transferring the mixture to a bowl. Set aside to cool.

To make 20 to 24 dumplings

1 cup cake flour
1 cup corn flour
¾ cup boiling water
2 tablespoons oil
⅓ cup minced onion
6 ounces ground pork
2 teaspoons salt
½ teaspoon pepper
1½ tablespoons sugar
3 tablespoons
   chopped, unsalted
   dry roasted peanuts
Lettuce leaves

STEAMED DUMPLINGS

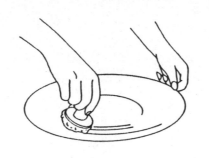

7. Oil a large plate. Oil the palms of your hands and pat about 1 tablespoon of dough into a 3-inch round. Make sure the center is thicker than the edge.

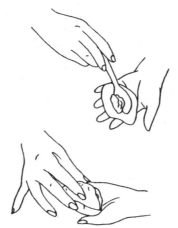

8. Place a teaspoon of pork mixture in the center of the dough and fold over.

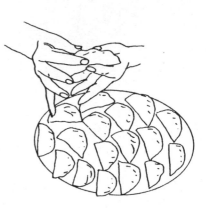

9. Pinch around the edge to seal. Place on the oiled plate. Repeat with the remaining ingredients.

10. Boil water in a steamer. Lay wet cheesecloth over the upper tray section to prevent dumplings from sticking.

11. Place the dumplings on the cheesecloth and steam for 15 minutes. Serve with crisp lettuce.

STUFFED BLACK MUSHROOMS

China

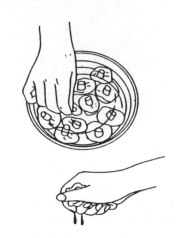

1. Soak the dried mushrooms in warm water until soft (about 30 minutes). Squeeze out the excess water. Cut off stems.

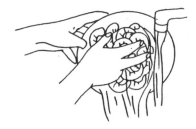

2. Shell and devein the shrimp. Put shrimp in a bowl with ½ teaspoon salt and gently mix with fingers. Rinse with several changes of water and drain well.

TECHNIQUES
Try to choose mushrooms of approximately the same size to allow uniform cooking.

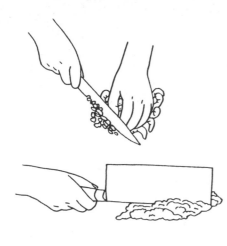

3. Mince shrimp, onion, coriander, and ginger root. Beat egg lightly.

4. Combine minced ingredients, egg, and all of the remaining stuffing ingredients in a bowl and mix thoroughly.

5. Fill the mushroom caps with stuffing, rounding off the tops. Garnish with coriander leaves.

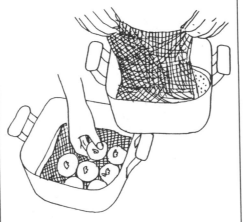

6. Boil water in the lower section of your steamer. Line the upper part with cheesecloth. Place the stuffed mushroom caps in the steamer and steam, covered, for 15 minutes. Serve warm.

To make 24

24 medium-size dried Chinese mushrooms

Stuffing
½ pound fresh shrimp
½ teaspoon salt
½ white onion, minced
¼ cup minced fresh coriander
1 teaspoon finely minced fresh ginger root
1 egg, lightly beaten
½ pound ground pork
½ teaspoon salt
1 teaspoon sesame seed oil
½ teaspoon pepper
1 tablespoon sherry
1 tablespoon oyster sauce

Coriander leaves for garnish

OVEN COOKED

CHICKEN LOAF

Japan

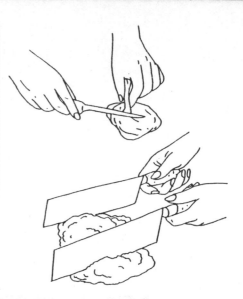

1. Bone the chicken thighs and mince the meat fine. A food processor should not be used for this step as the meat may lose its texture. Most Oriental chefs use two cleavers or two large knives.

2. Add all remaining ingredients except oil and mix well until a pastelike consistency is achieved.

3. Brush oil on a cookie sheet. Spread the mixture evenly, about ⅓-inch thick over the sheet.

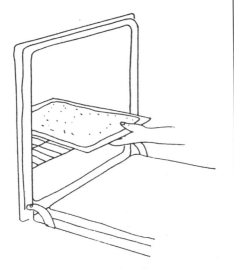

4. Preheat your oven to 400° F. Place the sheet on the center shelf and bake for 15 minutes. Move the sheet to the top shelf and turn the heat up to broil. Broil for two minutes, or until the top is golden brown. Take care that the fat from the chicken does not catch fire.

5. Remove and lift the loaf onto a double thickness of paper towel to drain excess fat. Cut into 1- × 1½-inch rectangles while hot. Cool and serve at room temperature.

To serve 8

1 pound chicken thighs
4 dried shiitake mushrooms, soaked in warm water until soft, then minced
½ cup minced scallions
⅓ cup minced carrots
2 teaspoons fresh ginger juice
2 eggs
1 cup Japanese style breadcrumbs (see Ingredients, page x)
4 teaspoons miso
2 tablespoons sake
Oil

CURRIED CASHEW NUTS

India

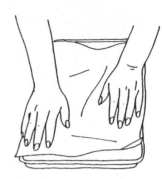

1. Preheat your oven to 250° F. Line a cookie sheet with brown paper.

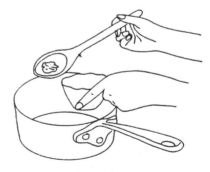

2. Crush a clove of garlic. Heat oil in a large saucepan and brown the garlic. Remove the garlic and discard.

3. Off heat, add soy sauce, curry powder, pepper, and salt. Heat over moderate heat. Add nuts and stir until they are thoroughly coated.

4. Remove the nuts and spread them on the lined cookie sheet. Bake for 10 minutes until they are lightly browned and crisp.

To make 2 cups

1 clove garlic, crushed
3 tablespoons peanut
   oil
1 tablespoon light soy
   sauce
1 tablespoon curry
   powder
¼ teaspoon white
   pepper
1 teaspoon salt
2 cups cashew nuts

GLAZED SPARERIBS

China

1. Combine the seasoning mixture ingredients and mix well. First coat both sides of the ribs with the mixture. Rub in well. Use the remainder of the mixture to further coat the meat side. Let stand in the refrigerator for 8 to 12 hours.

2. Preheat oven to 450° F. Place a turkey rack flat on a shallow baking pan and oil the rack. Mix glaze.

3. Scrape off the seasoning mixture and place the ribs on the rack. Brush on glaze.

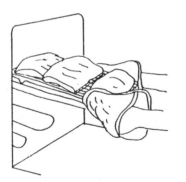

4. Place ribs in the oven and immediately turn the heat down to 425° F. Roast for 30 minutes, basting occasionally with glaze. Decrease the heat again, to 325° F., and roast for another 30 minutes. Baste occasionally.

5. Remove from the oven and let stand for 15 minutes. Cut the ribs into one rib pieces and serve.

To make about 24

Seasoning Mixture
1 cup sugar
1 teaspoon salt
1 teaspoon saltpeter
   (optional)

3 backribs (have
   butcher crack bones)

Glaze
2 tablespoons honey
5 teaspoons ground
   bean sauce
5 teaspoons hoisin
   sauce
2 teaspoons garlic
   purée
1 tablespoon dry sherry
5 teaspoons soy sauce
1 tablespoon catsup

OVEN-BROILED OYSTERS

Japan

1. To clean the oysters, place them in a bowl and add flour. Mix thoroughly. Then rinse under cold water and drain.

2. Mince onion and combine with soy sauce and sake in a bowl. Add the oysters and coat thoroughly. Set aside to marinate for 15 minutes.

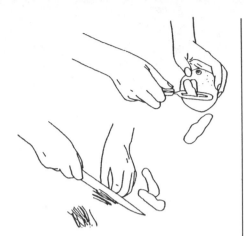

3. Wash a lemon. With a vegetable peeler, peel the skin into long strips. Shred into needle thin pieces.

5. Place on a serving plate and sprinkle with shredded lemon.

To make 24

24 small oysters
1 tablespoon flour
2 tablespoons finely
minced onion
¼ cup soy sauce
1½ tablespoons sake
2 tablespoons lemon
rind, thinly shredded
Oil

4. Heat oven broiler. Oil a shallow baking pan lightly and lay oysters out in a single layer. Place the baking pan in the top quarter of the pre-heated oven and broil for about 4 minutes. Turn oysters and broil for an additional 4 minutes.

OTHERS

BROCCOLI WITH SOY DIP

Japan

1. Cut and separate broccoli into florets. Wash and drain.

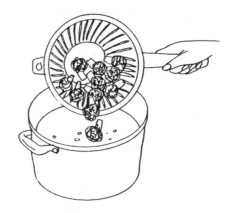

2. Over high heat, bring 2 quarts of water to boil. Add salt and oil. Add broccoli and bring water back to boil. Cook for 2 minutes without a cover. Remove broccoli with a strainer and immediately plunge into cold water to prevent further cooking. Drain well.

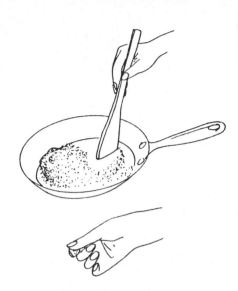

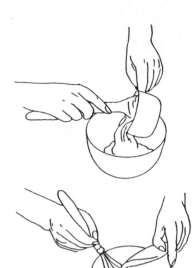

Serves 8

2 bunches of broccoli
1 tablespoon salt
1 tablespoon peanut oil

Dip
3 tablespoons white
   sesame seeds,
   toasted and crushed
1 cup mayonnaise
2 tablespoons soy
   sauce
3 tablespoons rice
   vinegar

3. Heat an 8-inch skillet over medium low heat. Add sesame seeds. Toast while stirring constantly. Do not overtoast or they will turn bitter. Toast until they turn golden or until a few seeds crushed between the thumb and forefinger begin to impart a fragrance.

5. Put mayonnaise into a bowl and stir in soy sauce and vinegar. Blend with a wire whisk. Add sesame seeds and blend well. Serve with the broccoli, at room temperature.

4. Remove the seeds and place in a mortar. Crush.

CHICKEN IN LETTUCE CUPS

China

1. Wash chicken thoroughly. Place the chicken breast side down in boiling chicken stock or water. Make sure that the chicken is completely submerged. Bring liquid back to boil and boil for 2 or 3 minutes. Lower the heat to simmer, and cover. Simmer for 20 minutes. Turn the heat off and let stand for about 2 hours. The chicken will continue to cook and then cool during this time.

2. Steps 2, 3, and 4 can be performed while chicken is poaching. Cut the head of lettuce in half and remove the leaves to make small cups. Cut if necessary. Place in plastic wrap and refrigerate until just before serving.

TECHNIQUES
Chinese chefs will insist that a large metal spoon be placed in the body cavity while boiling the chicken to improve heat distribution. It is important to use fresh oil in Step 7. The rice noodles will pick up any old flavors.

3. Chop the peanuts coarsely. Wash coriander and pat dry with a paper towel. Then chop in 1-inch lengths. Discard tough stems.

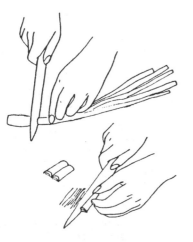

4. Cut the white part of the scallion in half lengthwise and julienne. Chop sweet/sour pickled onion coarsely.

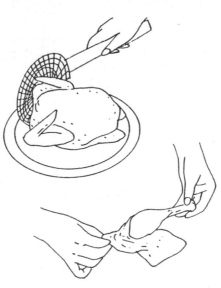

5. Remove the chicken from the broth. Save the broth for other recipes. It may be frozen. Peel the skin from the chicken and discard.

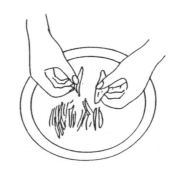

6. Pick the meat from the chicken and shred to pencil size thickness.

To make 48

1 3- to 3½-pound fryer
Chicken stock or water
   to cover chicken
½ head of iceberg
   lettuce
1 cup unsalted dry
   roasted peanuts
1 bunch fresh coriander
4 scallions (use 2½
   inches of the white
   part only)
10 sweet/sour pickled
   onions, chopped
Fresh oil
2 ounces rice noodles

Dressing
¼ cup precooked
   peanut oil
2 teaspoons Five Spice
   Salt (see page 136)
2 teaspoons powdered
   hot mustard, mixed
   with water to soft
   paste

CHICKEN IN LETTUCE CUPS

7. Heat 4 inches of fresh oil in a wok to 325° F. Drop a small bunch of rice noodles into hot oil. Almost instantly the noodles will swell to several times their original size. Remove right away and drain on several layers of paper towel. Cook remaining noodles.

8. Gently crush the noodles until they are about 1 inch in length. This can be done between two pieces of paper towel.

9. To precook the peanut oil, heat it to smoking and then cool. Prepare Five Spice Salt (page 136). Mix mustard. Put these together in a large salad bowl and mix thoroughly.

10. Add the chicken and toss well to coat with the dressing.

11. Add the crushed rice noodles, peanuts, coriander, scallion, and sweet/sour onions and toss thoroughly. Serve with lettuce cups on the side. A bit of chicken mixture is spooned into the lettuce, which is rolled and eaten like a tortilla.

CUCUMBER WITH CRAB

Japan

1. Cut cucumbers into 3-inch segments. Core with zucchini corer, taking care to leave nice circular centers.

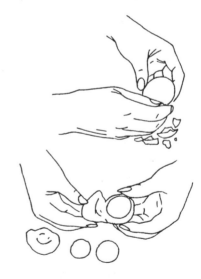

2. Hard-boil eggs and separate into whites and yolks.

TECHNIQUES
An alternative method is to cut the cucumber into ⅜-inch slices. Then, with a round hole cutter, punch out the center of each slice. Stuff all slices (keeping them flat on the table top). This method produces a neater appetizer.

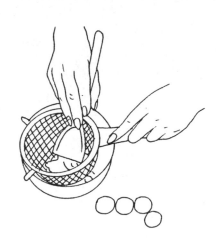

3. Force 2 egg whites and 6 yolks through a fine sieve, twice.

4. Mince crabmeat and pickled onions and add to eggs. Add salt and lemon juice. Mix well to blend thoroughly.

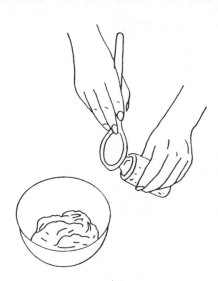

5. Correct seasoning to your taste. Stuff cucumbers as shown.

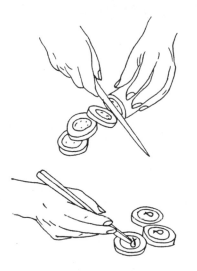

6. Cut cucumber segments into slices about ⅜ inch thick. Top each with pickled ginger and serve.

To make about 30

1 thin English cucumber
6 eggs
⅔ cup cooked
   crabmeat
7 sweet/sour pickled
   onions
¾ tablespoon salt
2 teaspoons lemon
   juice
Pickled ginger root

119

CUCUMBER WITH WALNUT MISO

Japan

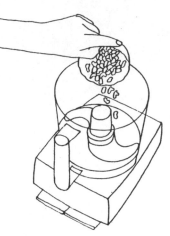

1. Mince walnuts. This can be done easily in a food processor, but be careful not to create a paste.

2. In a saucepan, combine miso, sugar, mirin, and sake. Cook over low heat while stirring constantly for 5 minutes.

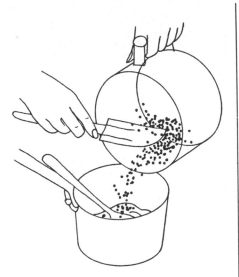

To make about 40

⅔ cup walnuts
½ cup red miso
¼ cup sugar
¼ cup mirin
2 tablespoons sake
1 English cucumber

3. Remove from the heat and stir in the walnuts. Set aside to cool.

5. Spoon a little miso and walnut mixture on each section. Top with a piece of walnut and serve.

4. Cut cucumber into 3-inch sections and core. Then cut into 1-inch sections and quarter each of these as shown.

ROLLED SASHIMI

Japan

1. In a small cup (sake cup) mix wasabi powder with a little cold water to make a soft paste. Then mix vigorously for a minute. Cover with plastic wrap and set aside.

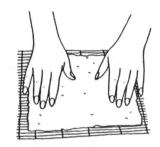

2. Lay a sheet of nori (seaweed) on top of a bamboo mat (maki sudare).

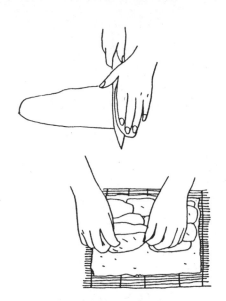

3. Make thin (¼-inch) slanted slices of fish and place in a layer on top of the nori. Cover completely.

4. Using your finger, spread a thin line of wasabi across the center.

5. Cut the green part of the scallions to the same length as the nori and lay a few across. Spread half of the pickled ginger alongside the scallion greens.

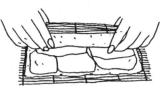

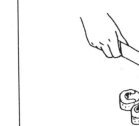

6. Using the bamboo mat to help you, roll up the nori. It will seal itself against the fish. Cut into ¾-inch slices and serve with soy sauce and wasabi or soy sauce mixed with lemon juice.

To make 24

2 teaspoons wasabi powder
2 sheets nori (seaweed)
1 pound fillet of very fresh halibut, yellowtail, or tuna
A bunch of very young scallions, green part only
¼ cup pickled ginger
Soy sauce
Wasabi powder
1 lemon (optional)

SEVICHE

Philippines

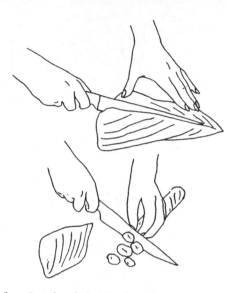

1. Cut the fish fillet into bite-size pieces.

TECHNIQUES
Take care to use a wooden or plastic spoon in Step 3. Metal will react with the citrus and impart an unpleasant taste.

Wash your hands, cutting board and knife after handling hot chilies. Oil from a hot chili can irritate the skin and easily get into the eyes.

2. Put the fish and salt in a bowl, and cover with lime juice.

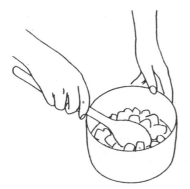

3. Toss gently with a wooden spoon. Refrigerate for at least 4 to 6 hours. Stir occasionally.

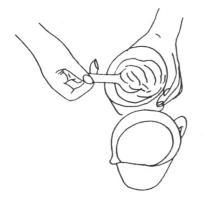

4. Combine coconut milk and sour cream and mix well until blended. Refrigerate for at least one hour.

5. Slice the onion into paper-thin slices. Put in a large bowl and add cold water to cover by at least 2 inches. Set aside for 10 minutes. Drain. Repeat twice more.

6. Drain fish and reserve the marinade.

Serves 8

1 pound fillet of red
   snapper or sea bass
1 teaspoon salt
½ cup lime juice
⅔ cup coconut milk
3 tablespoons sour
   cream
½ medium white onion
1 green chili, toasted,
   skinned, and minced
   (optional)
1 medium tomato
5 or 6 sprigs coriander,
   leaves only
Lettuce for serving

125

SEVICHE

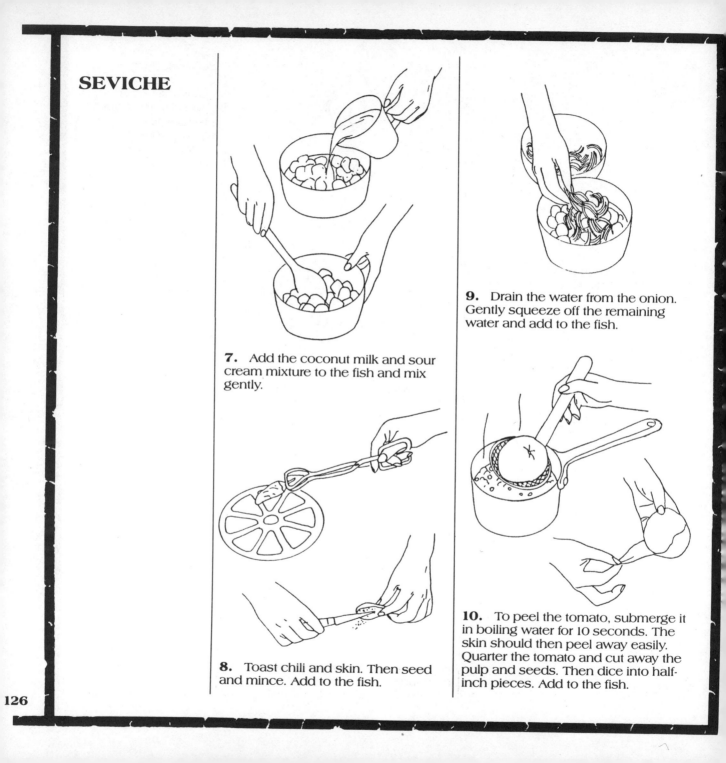

7. Add the coconut milk and sour cream mixture to the fish and mix gently.

8. Toast chili and skin. Then seed and mince. Add to the fish.

9. Drain the water from the onion. Gently squeeze off the remaining water and add to the fish.

10. To peel the tomato, submerge it in boiling water for 10 seconds. The skin should then peel away easily. Quarter the tomato and cut away the pulp and seeds. Then dice into half-inch pieces. Add to the fish.

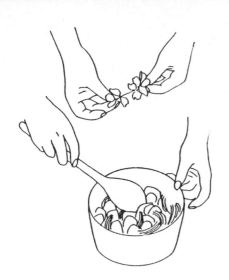

11. Pinch the leaves off the stems of coriander and add. Discard stems. Toss the mixture gently but thoroughly with a wooden spoon. Taste for flavor. Add a little reserved marinade if you feel it needs it. Serve on a bed of crisp lettuce.

SAUCES, DIPS, AND DOUGH

CHILI OIL

China

1. Tie scallion in a loose knot. This will make it easier to insert and remove from the oil.

2. Smash ginger root with a mallet.

5. Strain the oil into a clean bottle.

To make 8 ounces

1 scallion
1 large ginger root,
  crushed
1 cup vegetable oil
⅓ cup dried chili,
  crushed

3. Heat oil in a saucepan until smoke starts to rise. Turn off the heat immediately and add scallion and ginger. Let it stand for 5 minutes. Remove scallion and ginger and discard. Cool oil for another 5 minutes.

4. Add the crushed chili to the oil and allow to steep overnight.

6. Place the chili in a covered jar. Both will keep indefinitely, though the oil should be refrigerated.

131

COCONUT MILK

Thailand

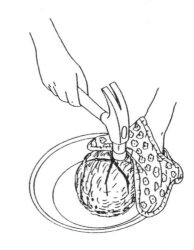

1. Shake the coconut before buying. Buy the one that sounds as though it has the most water. With a hammer and nail, pierce the three indentations at the flat end. Drain off the water.

2. Place the coconut on a cookie sheet and bake in a preheated 350° F. oven until the shell cracks—about 20 to 30 minutes. Remove the coconut and crack further with a hammer.

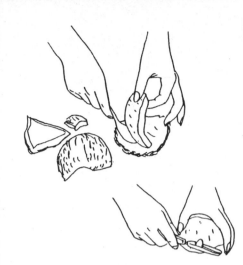

3. Pry the meat away from the shell. Peel off the brown skin with a vegetable peeler.

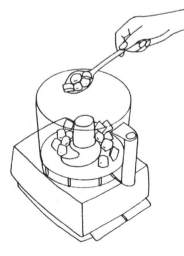

4. Cut the white into small pieces. Using the steel blade, chop them fine in a food processor.

5. Put the chopped coconut in a bowl and pour boiling water over it. Let it steep for 20 minutes.

6. Pour the mixture into another bowl through a double layer of cheesecloth. Squeeze hard to extract as much liquid as possible. Discard the pulp. Coconut milk will turn rancid after about 1 week in the refrigerator, so the unused portion should always be frozen.

To make about 1½ cups

1 coconut
1 cup boiling water

133

CRUNCHY PEANUT SAUCE

Indonesia

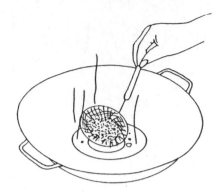

1. Heat oil in a wok. Put dried onion flakes in a small wire mesh strainer and lower into oil. Fry until they are golden brown, about 20 seconds. Drain on a paper towel. Do the same to minced garlic (about 3 minutes) and crushed chili (about 20 seconds). Drain on a paper towel.

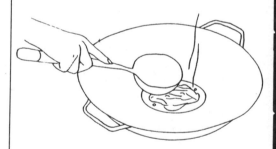

2. In the remaining oil, fry shrimp paste over low heat for 2 minutes while crushing it with a spatula. Add lime juice and soy sauce.

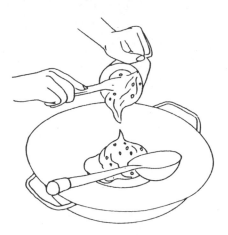

3. Off heat add palm sugar and peanut butter and mix well.

4. Add cooked onion from step one. Crumble it with your fingers as you are adding. Add garlic and chili. You may prepare the sauce up to this point ahead of time. Keep it refrigerated in a covered bowl.

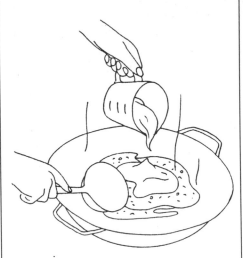

5. Just before serving, warm peanut mixture over low heat. Add coconut milk and mix well to blend. Be careful not to overheat. This will cause the milk to separate. Serve as a dip for fresh and parboiled vegetables. Use as a base for Satay Sauce (page 73).

To make about 3 cups

½ cup peanut oil
1 tablespoon dehydrated, minced onions
5 cloves garlic, minced fine
1½ tablespoons crushed chili
1 teaspoon dried shrimp paste
1 tablespoon lime juice
1 tablespoon soy sauce
1 tablespoon palm sugar
1 cup crunchy peanut butter (unsalted)
1 cup coconut milk

FIVE SPICE SALT

China

1. Heat wok over low heat and add salt. Stir salt constantly until it turns slightly brown. This should take about 5 minutes. Turn off the heat and allow it to cool for about 5 minutes.

2. Add five spice powder and mix well.

3. When completely cool, put into a glass jar with a screw top. The salt will keep several months and may be used as a table salt or as a dip for Five Spice Spareribs.

SHRIMP SAUCE

Thailand

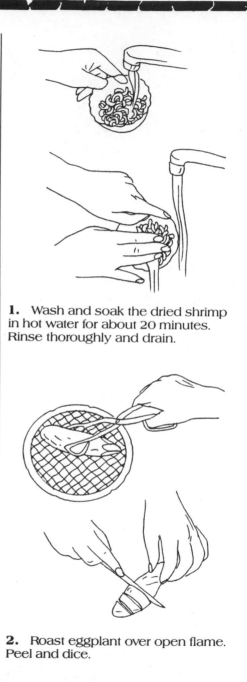

1. Wash and soak the dried shrimp in hot water for about 20 minutes. Rinse thoroughly and drain.

2. Roast eggplant over open flame. Peel and dice.

3. Wrap kapi in foil and grill 2 minutes on each side.

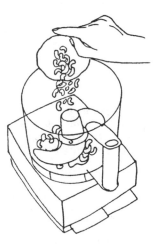

4. Combine all ingredients in a food processor and process until smooth, about 2 minutes. Scrape down the sides of bowl as needed.

5. Pour into serving bowl. This shrimp sauce can be served as a dip for raw or partially cooked vegetables, cooked prawns, or shrimp. In Thailand it is used as a seasoning for practically everything.

To make about 1 cup

2 tablespoons dried shrimp
1 Japanese eggplant (or ⅓ Italian eggplant)
1 teaspoon dried shrimp paste (kapi)
7 cloves garlic, crushed
2 teaspoons crushed chili
2 teaspoons palm sugar
2 tablespoons lime juice
1½ tablespoons soy sauce
3 tablespoons water
1 tablespoon fish sauce (nam pla)

FUN GOR/HAR GOW DOUGH

China

1. Sift wheat starch and tapioca flour separately into a bowl. Then sift them together.

2. Gradually pour 1¼ cups boiling water into the mixture. Mix well so that the dough will be partially cooked. Add a little more water if needed.

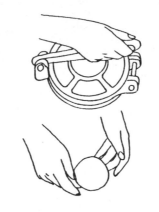

To make about 48

1¼ cups wheat starch
¾ cup tapioca starch
1¼ cups boiling water
1 tablespoon lard
Oil

3. Stir in the lard. Cover and set aside for 15 minutes or until cool enough to handle. Knead the dough for 5 minutes. It should be soft and smooth. Cover and let it rest for 10 minutes.

5. Roll out each piece to make a 2½-inch-diameter round disk. A tortilla press can be used to do this job. Oil both halves of the press. Cover the disks to prevent drying out. They are to be used as wrappers for the Fun Gor and Har Gow dumplings.

4. Divide the dough in half. Lightly oil a work surface. Knead one of the halves for 2 more minutes and roll out into a long cylinder about 1 inch in diameter. Cut into ½-inch pieces. Cover to prevent drying out. Do the same with the second half.

INDEX